THE GOSPEL
of the
40 DAYS

Gordon Kenworthy Reed

THE GOSPEL OF THE 40 DAYS
by Gordon Kenworthy Reed

Copyright © 2018 by Tanglewood Publishing

ISBN-13: 978-0-9972490-5-7

All rights reserved. No part of this book may be reproduced
in any from without written permission from

Tanglewood Publishing
800-241-4016
www.tanglewoodpublishing.org

Book Design and Layout by Capsicum Designs, Mieke Moller
Cover Design by Christy Rodriguez

Painting: *The Pilgrims on the Emmaus Road* by James Tissot

Printed in the United States of America

Table of Contents

Introduction
1. Saved by Grace, Known by Name 1
2. Easter Joy 9
3. Forty Indispensable Days 17
4. The Emmaus Road 25
5. Unforgettable Encounter 33
6. Celebrating the Ascension of Christ 41
7. The Lamb Upon the Throne 49
8. Salvaging a Fallen Saint 59
9. Thomas the Believer 67
10. The Missionary Mandate 75
11. Words of Love and Great Power 83
12. This Same Jesus Shall Return 89
13. The Judge of All the Earth 97
14. Postscript 107

Introduction

I believe that the most overlooked and under-preached sections of the New Testament are the records we have in all four of the Gospels concerning the forty days after our Lord Jesus rose from the dead and before He ascended to His rightful throne. The records are there for all to read, but in the thrill of the resurrection, and the amazing wonder of His ascension, somehow, we have ignored the importance of what our Lord taught during those forty indispensable days of glory.

When the Lord was resurrected from the dead, a corner in time was turned, and nothing would ever be the same again on planet earth. Just as sin had once fundamentally altered both the creation and the human race, so another fundamental alteration took place at the resurrection of our Lord. After the Lord came back from the dead and presented Himself alive to His disciples, He spent forty days interpreting to them by word the meaning of this mighty act of God. As you look back over the Bible, you discover this is the usual pattern of revelation. God acts in a mighty way, and then by His spoken words to and through His chosen messengers,

He gives light and understanding concerning His great work. One example of this is seen in Exodus. As Moses was tending the sheep of his father-in-law, suddenly he saw a strange and wonderful sight. There on yonder mountain side was a bush burning brightly but not being consumed. As he drew near to see the strange sight, the voice of the Lord spoke out of the burning bush, and Moses was called to serve God and His people.

Another even more striking example would be the crossing of the Red Sea. The waters of the sea parted before the trapped Israelites who were being pursued by Pharaoh's army. At the word of the Lord, Moses held his staff over the waters, and a parting was made for Israel to escape dry shod, while the pursuing Egyptians were drowned when they attempted to follow. From that moment on, this mighty deed of God became the centerpiece of God's redemptive revelation. Moses continually reminded Israel of God's saving grace as seen in this grand event. The prophets who followed Moses often harkened back to this event and would exhort the people to faith and faithfulness by recalling God's miraculous mercy.

So the teachings of Christ during those missing forty days loom large on the horizon of revelation. This body of teaching provides the link between the ministry of Jesus Christ and the coming of the Holy Spirit to begin His work. Before and even after the resurrection the disciples were "foolish and slow of heart to believe all that the prophets had spoken concerning Christ." But by the time Peter preached his powerful and famous sermon on the day of Pentecost, by which three thousand were brought into the kingdom, it is obvious the disciples had a clear and full grasp of the meaning of Scripture, especially as it relates to the person and work of Christ. This was not only because the promise of the Spirit had been fulfilled, but also because of what Christ had taught them concerning Himself during those forty wonderful days. Those teachings also added boldness and a level of assurance which enabled His disciples to carry out the great commission and to live by the great commandment.

It would be impossible in one short book or even a lengthy time to explore in full all that the Lord Jesus taught us during those glory days after His resurrection and before His ascension, but I will briefly summarize these things so we might see something of the power of Christ's teachings in that all-too-short time span. What were these great truths which transformed His disciples and made them such powerful transformers?

The late Dr. Williams Childs Robinson coined a phrase referring to the teachings of our Lord during the forty days between His resurrection and His ascension into heaven. He called it "the Gospel of the Forty Days" and noted the neglect in most preaching of this important link in Scripture. During those glorious days, the Lord Jesus laid the foundation for understanding the Old Testament and for writing of the New Testament. It is no exaggeration to say that during these forty days, He planted the seed for every major doctrine found in the entire New Testament. First of all, He showed Himself alive with many infallible proofs of His resurrection, its reality, and its meaning for believers. This would be the foundation stone for every sermon recorded in the book of Acts. In every epistle inspired by the Holy Spirit and written by the apostles, the fact and meaning of Christ's death and resurrection shine through their pages with hope and great joy. Here also we see the great truth of God's amazing sovereignty: His foreordaining whatsoever comes to pass to His own glory. During this time He gave to us the missionary mandate and the baptismal formula. He renewed His promise of the Holy Spirit who would shortly come upon the disciples and the church they would plant. He taught them He would soon ascend to the Father's right hand to reign over the church, and at the Father's word would come again to receive His own to Himself, judging the living and the dead.

1

Saved by Grace, Known by Name

~

JOHN 20:11-18

After His resurrection, the Lord Jesus spent forty days on earth before His ascension into heaven and return to glory. It was a transition time for His disciples, preparing them for His physical absence, and also preparing them for the great work He would give them to do. During this time He appeared to various people. He revealed Himself as the risen Lord to His mother and His earthly brothers and sisters, who as yet had not accepted His claim to be God's Son and Messiah. He also appeared to gatherings of His disciples, even as many as five hundred at one time. But the most powerful and deeply touching of all His recorded appearances were His encounters with a few individuals whom He singled out for special attention. Perhaps the most touching and beautiful was His speaking to Mary Magdalene, just outside the tomb.

But why should any of these encounters between the risen Christ and His followers of old be of any concern for us? The answer is simple. In all of these people and their experiences for good or bad, we see ourselves as if in a mirror. Their fears are our fears. Their disappointments and heartaches are ours. And their redeeming and healing experiences with the risen Lord may be ours too, for the common denominator is faith: faith in the person, word, and works of Jesus Christ, the Son of God, the Savior of sinners.

How, where, and when Mary of Magdala first came to know and follow the Lord Jesus none of the Gospel writers tell us. The only thing we know about her salvation is that she had been demon-possessed at one time and the Lord Jesus had set her free from that bondage. From then on she was a devoted follower and disciple of His. She was from the little lake village of Magdala, hence the title Mary Magdalene. This was to distinguish her from several other Marys who also knew and loved the Lord. Let's look at Mary's past as we can put it together from what we know.

I. MARY'S PAST

A. Before Christ Found and Saved Her

She probably was born and grew up in the Galilean village of Magdala, on the western shore of the lake. The culture was that of first century Galilee, which by then was a province of the Roman Empire, north of Samaria. But the people were largely Jewish and had deep ties with Judea to the south. Although influenced by Greek culture, which was introduced during the conquests of Alexander the Great centuries before the Roman invasion, still the Galileans were for the most part loyal to their Jewish roots, retaining their own language, Aramaic, which was very similar to the ancient Hebrew. Greek was the official language but the people spoke in their native tongue. So Mary's name in her own language was Miriam. That's what her mother called her, and her friends with whom she grew up, and that's what Jesus called her too.

From what Luke tells us in his Gospel, she was a friend of Joanna, who was the wife of Herod's chief officer. This could well indicate that she may have been a woman of some wealth, and may have been a widow. Again the details of her early life are sketchy at best, but this much we know: she had been overcome by evil at some point in her life. Demonic control does not just happen. It occurs when evil is endured, then embraced. Mary moved in high company, and might have been caught up in the decadent and sinful lifestyle often associated with the affluent of that time (and our time too). All of this is mere reasonable assumption, but at some point we do know that Satan took control of her life. She was lost and without God and hope. Then Jesus came.

B. Her Life as a Believer

When the Lord came into her life, evil was cast out. Then, along with her close friends, Joanna and Susanna, she became a devout disciple of Jesus, even giving what she had to provide for His earthly needs, as evidence of her changed life. She had obviously made a clean break with her old life. That is how it was then and always must be. No one can serve two masters, no matter how you may try. Since her salvation came early in the ministry of Jesus, she had the better part of three years to follow Him, learn His teaching, and witness His miracles. She was convinced that He was indeed the Christ, the Son of God, the Savior of the world.

II. MARY'S HEARTBREAK AND DEEP GRIEF

Then her world fell apart. In spite of Jesus' great popularity among the common people, the jealousy and anger of the rulers and leaders had reached a boiling point. The triumphant ride of Jesus into the Holy city to the acclaim of the multitudes was followed by scheming and plotting of these leaders to have Him killed. No doubt Mary and her friends had come to Jerusalem from Magdala to observe Passover. She would know that Jesus and the inner circle of twelve would be celebrating the feast together. Then word began to spread that He had been betrayed, arrested, condemned by the Jewish Sanhedrin, and turned over to the Romans with a demand for His execution. Unbelievably, the Romans had acquiesced, though knowing He was innocent. In growing horror, Mary, along with Jesus' mother, His best friend John, and a few other women, bravely followed the mob to the place of execution; and right there before her tear-filled eyes and breaking heart she saw them nail Him to the cross and lift Him up to die. She heard the mocking of the Pharisees and priests who had come to gloat over Him. She shared the unbelievable grief along with His mother of seeing Him suddenly slump and die and saw the soldier thrust a spear into His heart to make sure He was really dead. She watched as Joseph and Nicodemus came and removed His dead body from the cross and place it in a newly hewn tomb. She carefully marked the spot, determined that after the Sabbath she would finish the work of preparing His body for its final burial. Then probably with her friends, and perhaps with Jesus' mother, she went to a hidden place to weep and mourn as she had never mourned before.

Why? Where was God? Why did He let His beloved Son die? She had hoped so much to see Him enthroned in Jerusalem and to bring in the new Kingdom He had promised. Her soul was engulfed in grief too deep for words and unassuaged by tears. The dark night of the soul is a dreadful thing to experience, and yet most of us have had such times when faith has at least wavered, when nothing made much sense, and God offered no explanation...at least not one we could accept or understand. Had Jesus really saved and forgiven her? Was the control of evil broken, or would Satan take control of her life again?

Early Sunday morning, with the passing of the Jewish Sabbath, Mary Magdalene and the other Mary came early to the tomb to do the final honors and make preparation for the permanent burial. They were totally unprepared for the final blow, the ultimate desecration. Someone had taken away His body! The tomb was opened, His body gone! She ran to tell Peter and John and blurted out her lament, "They have taken away His body, and we do not know where they have laid Him." As best she could, she tried to follow the running men back to the tomb, but when she arrived, they were running frantically away, leaving her alone with the final grief. She who had left all to follow Him, and given all to clothe and feed Him, would not be allowed to do for Him the final touch of honor and love. It was just too much to bear.

III. MARY MAGDALENE, MEET AGAIN YOUR BELOVED TEACHER AND YOUR GOD

As Mary wept, she just had to look into the tomb one more time to make sure His body was really not there. Looking in, she saw a strange sight: two angels clothed in white sitting on the shelf where the body had lain. They asked her why she was weeping and she explained, "Because they have taken away my Lord, and I do not know where they have laid Him." While she was speaking, she turned from the grave and sensed someone standing just behind her who asked her the same question, but added "Whom are you seeking?" Thinking he was the caretaker of the cemetery she said, "Sir, if you have taken Him away, tell me where you have laid Him and I will take Him away."

Then Jesus spoke her name in her native language, even as she had heard Him call her out of sin and bondage three years before. Just "Miriam." That was all. But it was enough. When He first spoke to her, she did not recognize His voice, but when He called her by name, she knew Him. That blessed, surprising joy awaits all the sheep of Jesus for whom He died and rose again. You will hear the voice of the Son of God, calling you by name, and then you will see Him and know Him. When she thought He was dead, she still called Him "My Lord," but now she added "Rabboni!" in Aramaic. This title was given to only a rare few rabbis, and was also used to address God in prayer. Falling at His feet Miriam adored and worshiped The Risen Savior. "Stop clinging to me Miriam, though I have not yet ascended to My Father, you go and tell My brethren that I am ascending to My Father and your Father, to My God and your God." And she did. With great excitement and joy, she ran to bring the good news.

She had gone to the tomb looking for a dead body to bury. She left proclaiming a risen, living Savior!

Now what may we learn from this, and how much of Mary's joy may we share?

1. Mary was assured that her salvation was real and permanent. Her Lord and Rabboni had not been defeated by evil and death, but had defeated them. So the power of evil which had once dominated her life could never again rule over her. Your assurance of forgiveness of sin and ultimate victory rests on the same truth Mary discovered… Christ is risen.

2. Mary learned that though she could not cling forever to the earthly Jesus, because He was ascending to the Father, He would be with her always; in this world by the Holy Spirit, and in Heaven as the conquering King and ever present Lord of glory. Now she would live in joy and blessed hope that neither trial nor circumstance could ever take away again. And you too may join her in that knowledge and joy.

3. Mary was given a task which would give her life meaning and purpose as she had never dreamed possible. "Go tell them what and whom you have seen." Above all lesser causes and callings in life of vocations or relationships, the one great purpose we share with Mary is to be faithful witnesses in life and word that our Lord Jesus died for our sins, took away our punishment, is risen and ascended, and reigns and rules in Heaven with the Father. And as Mary and the others were later told, "He is coming again."

4. You may be saying, "If only I could hear Him call my name." You have, and you will! So go forth with something of the same eager joy to share the good news with one and all. And the joy of Miriam of Magdala will be yours.

For Discussion and Reflection

1. We read in this chapter that the post-Resurrection encounters between Jesus and specially selected individuals are of personal significance to us because we see ourselves in each of them. Using the previous discussion and John 20:11-18 for reference, consider how you are like Mary Magdalene. What traits of hers do you see when you look in the mirror, or when you reflect upon the ways in which you have gone astray, or when you look back upon the various turning points in your life?

2. After pondering your kinship with Mary, perhaps challenge yourself to work through the same exercise with others who experienced a personal encounter with Jesus after His resurrection: two disciples on the road to Emmaus (Luke 24:13-35), the disciples in the upper room (John 20:19-23, Luke 24:36-48), and Thomas (John 20:24-28).

3. We are assured that Jesus has indeed called our name, just as He called Mary Magdalene's. Can you recall a time that you knew with certainty He was calling you by name? If not, can you recall a time that He likely was calling but you were not able to hear? In either case, how did you respond? How might you have responded differently? Did the experience change how you listen for His voice in your life now? What might put you in a mindset to be more expectant of and attentive to His call?

4. When Jesus called Mary by name, she recognized Him and believed. What has convinced you of the reality of the risen Christ? How would you explain the reason for your faith to an unbeliever?

2

Easter Joy

∼

JOHN 20

From the book of Hebrews we read these words concerning our Lord and His resurrection from the dead: "...who for the joy that was set before Him, endured the cross, despising the shame, and is set down at the right hand of the throne of God."

Easter is a season of great joy! The strong sense of spring is all around us, and the renewal of life in nature grows stronger each day. The sun's rays grow brighter and warmer. All around us we see and hear the birds begin the overture of spring's beautiful symphony. Flowers are in bloom everywhere, fish are biting, (at least for some of us), and in general the world is waking up after its winter's sleep.

The setting of early spring makes Easter seem somehow more real and joyful. All around we see nature's glorious allegory of the resurrection. The undeniable historicity of the empty tomb beckons us to come and see its silent but eloquent witness to the central truth of the Christian faith. Once again it seems our ears pick up the incredible cry, "HE IS RISEN!" and spontaneously we echo back, HE IS RISEN INDEED!"

As we read the Gospels' accounts of the resurrection, the note of incredible joy dominates. And the verse from Hebrews with which I began this message sums up the whole mood of the season. It was the joy of the anticipated resurrection and ascension which gave Christ the courage to face the cross with all its agony and shame. The mountaintop of joy towered over the deep valley of His sorrow and death.

For us today, the same motivation enables us to hear Christ calling, "Take up your cross and follow Me." We need to recapture our deep conviction of the reality of the resurrection, that we might once more be captivated by the exuberant joy our Lord experienced when He came forth from the grave. The more we come to understand the certainty of His resurrection, and participate in the Easter joy, the more we will be equipped to face the often harsh realities of life and the certainty of death.

I. FIRST, THERE WAS THE JOY OF BOTH GOD THE FATHER AND GOD THE SON

What joy there must have been in heaven when "Christ arose a victor o'er the dark domain." Can you even begin to imagine the joy of the Father when God the Son in the person of Jesus actually came forth from the grave? What breathtaking, lovely, and thrilling anthems must have resounded throughout heaven!

Consider the joy of the risen Christ Himself when He shook off the cloak of death and emerged from the rock-hewn tomb. The morning stars still shone brightly in the pre-dawn beauty of Easter morning. The eastern sky had just begun to blush ever so slightly. What joy must have been His at His wakening! His body first stirred. He sat up. Then He stood as the grave clothes fell away. For the first time in the history of the human race, living man experienced the fullness of the resurrection. This was not merely a resuscitation to mortality like Lazarus, but the glorious transformation, the glorious metamorphism into the body eternal and incorruptible. He was truly alive, as no other human being had ever been alive before. Death was behind Him once and for all. It is appointed unto man once to die, and so He did, but not forever, and not for long. He would say of Himself in the book of Revelation, "I am He who lives and was dead, and behold, I am alive forevermore." The tomb could not hold Him, because, in the words of Peter's great Pentecost sermon, "it is not possible that He should be held by it." So He stepped out to greet the happiest dawn since creation.

HIS WAS THE JOY OF VICTORY. He had fought the good fight and had won over the unbeatable foe. For the first time the human race knew victory over its final and most powerful foe... death. He won a victory never won before, and that humanity had despaired of ever winning; and not just for Himself alone, for He was the Second Adam, the federal head of a new humanity. "For as in Adam all die, even so in Christ shall all be made alive." "He is the firstborn among many brethren, the first fruits of them that sleep."

HIS WAS THE JOY OF ACCOMPLISHMENT. He had finished the work the Father had given Him to do. He had completed successfully the task which He had assumed from before the foundation of the world. He had won salvation for a great host which no man can number. He who had been condemned before the highest courts of humanity was now vindicated before the Father. He fulfilled the purpose for His advent. The pain, suffering, and humiliation of 33 years was now over. The song the angels sang at His birth will be sung throughout eternity in the new heavens and the new earth, "Peace on earth, good will towards men."

HIS WAS THE JOY OF PEACE. The battles had been fought, the war had been won. "The strife is o'er, the battle done, the victory of life is won. The song of triumph has begun. Alleluia!" Now peace has been made between the Creator and the creature rebel.

Christ having fought the deadly battle has made permanent peace for all those for whom He died.

II. THE JOY OF THE FIRST DISCIPLES

Christ's joy could not be complete until He had lifted the cloud of sorrow from off His loved ones. At first they were stunned by the empty tomb and filled with doubts. It was too good to be true! They were timid and frightened; they could scarcely believe their eyes and ears. But finally the truth overwhelmed them. He really had risen from the dead, even as He said He would. Not only was the tomb empty, He was in their midst talking with them, eating with them, and loving them as before.

There was the joy of Mary in the garden. She was weeping bitterly, for apparently His death did not satisfy His enemies; they had to steal His body also. Then one drew near to enquire into the reason for her grief and spoke her name. It was enough. She knew Him. He lived. She turned, she saw, she believed, she worshiped. She ran to tell His disciples.

There was the joy of Peter and John, who ran to the tomb upon hearing Mary's witness. Not that they didn't believe her report at first, but they just had to see. For Peter it meant possibly one more chance to show Jesus he really did love Him. For John the rediscovery of hope and the discovery of the ultimate truth and reality of the Word made flesh.

There was the joy of Mary His mother. Of that we are told nothing, nor do we need any word of her to imagine the joy and comfort she experienced when she saw her beloved Son alive again, who now was her beloved Lord to be worshiped.

Years ago a father took his young son sailing on Lake Michigan on a calm summer day. They sailed out of sight of land, only to be overtaken by a sudden fierce storm. Both were washed overboard, and the little craft sank beneath the giant waves. The grieving father was rescued by the coast guard. His last sight of his son had been watching the lad carried away from him clinging to a life vest. He was taken half conscious into the cabin of the cutter, and there in the next bunk was his son, returned as it were from a watery death. His joy was unbounded.

So must have been Mary's when she saw Jesus alive again. She had watched Him die in agony on the cross, but now He was alive; He was alive, that was enough.

III. THE JOY EASTER OFFERS TO US

Today, ours is the same sort of joy as was theirs who experienced the first Easter. Ours is the joy of freedom and release. The prison doors of our captivity to sin and death have been opened by our great Deliverer. At long last we may breathe the sweet air of freedom from condemnation, "for there is therefore now no condemnation to those who are in Christ Jesus." The darkness of deep night is over, and the light of the gospel now shines in our hearts, as the risen Christ sets us free and pardons all our sin.

Christ's resurrection is God's proof that His death was not in vain, and that our sins have been purged away forever. It is God's testimony that our debt is fully paid and that His love has redeemed us.

Ours is also the joy of anticipation. We know we have yet to see the full and final fruit of our Lord's resurrection from the dead. But we anchor our souls in the sure and certain hope of the resurrection of our own redeemed bodies, and a blessed reunion with our beloved dead in Christ. We live in the assurance that all sickness, sorrow, separation, pain and tears, and yes, even death itself must surrender to the invincible power of Christ's resurrection. Our future is bright with hope of a final Easter when the dead in Christ shall rise to be reunited, soul and body, with Christ and those whom He has redeemed. All creation groans and labors, awaiting the full redemption, the regeneration of all things in a glorious new creation, with Christ as the head of the new humanity. The joy of Easter today will be gloriously fulfilled in the Easter which shall be when He comes again. For now it is enough to know Christ is risen! He is risen indeed!

For Discussion and Reflection

1. How has the message of Jesus' resurrection brought joy into your life? Have you had opportunity to help others realize joy in their life because of who Jesus is and what he has done for them?

2. John 20 is the focus of this chapter about Easter joy. When reading this passage through verse 18, what words, actions, descriptions, or themes catch your attention as communicating a sense of joy? How would you describe the shift in mood from verse 1 to verse 18?

3. How does the assurance of the final Easter, resplendent in eternal joy, sustain you in your walk of faith?

4. Consider the joyous celebrations that occur in our culture at Christmastime, New Year's, and even birthdays. How do these celebrations compare with our celebration of the Resurrection? What does it say about our culture that we don't get as excited about this most significant event in human history? What does it say about our churches? What does it say about you? What needs to change in us to refocus our priorities and increase our excitement about the Resurrection?

3

Forty Indispensable Days of Glory

∼

LUKE 24:13-53

There were five things which Jesus emphasized during these forty wonderful days He spent with His disciples after His resurrection and before His ascension to heaven. These five teachings comprise the core doctrines that the church would proclaim by word and practice even to this very day. What were they, and why were they so important and remain so until the Lord returns in power and great glory?

FIRST IN IMPORTANCE WAS THE NECESSITY AND EFFICACY OF HIS DEATH ON THE CROSS

In many ways this was the first and most important of all Christ's post-resurrection teachings. His death on the cross seemed to be the one terrible contradiction in their minds. That the Son of God, the promised Messiah, the heir of David's throne should die in such an ignoble way at the hands of wicked men, was utterly incomprehensible. Before His death, the Lord had spoken often of this coming event, but the disciples refused to believe it could really happen. In fact the first time Jesus told them this, Peter took Him aside and began to rebuke Him saying, "Far be this from You Lord, this shall not happen to You!"

Now they were eager to listen and learn the meaning of His death, for they could not deny He had been crucified any more than they could deny He was alive again. It is from the words of Jesus during this time that we begin to understand the doctrine of the substitutionary atonement. Combine the words of Jesus with the later teaching of the Apostles, and this doctrine is set forth in all its glorious detail and saving power. The Lord Jesus explained to the two men on the Emmaus road the Old Testament Scriptures which spoke of His death as an offering for sin, thus showing that Christ's offering had been predicted both by the whole system of sacrifice in the law of Moses, as well as the many words of the later prophets, especially Isaiah.

His death was no accident, nor was it the result merely of men's hatred, but it was the foreordained will of God. This truth explained by the Lord to His disciples became the foundation for the Pentecost sermon of Peter, and indeed for all the preaching and writing of the Apostles.

When the evangelist Phillip led the Ethiopian eunuch to faith in Christ, he did so by explaining to him that Isaiah 53 was a description of Christ's death, and the meaning of this death for salvation. When Paul summed up the Gospel in I Corinthians 15, he wrote that Christ died for our sins according to the Scriptures of the Old Testament. So our understanding of the meaning of Christ's death flows out of the "Gospel of the forty days." By our Lord's own words we understand that He died for our sins, and by doing this won our salvation.

EQUALLY IMPORTANT HE TAUGHT THEM BY WORD AND DEED THE REALITY, THE NATURE, AND MEANING OF HIS RESURRECTION

The Lord did not bear witness to His own resurrection with just a few, fleeting, ghost-like appearances to one or two women and a few close disciples. Rather, for forty days He showed Himself alive with many infallible proofs. At one point He appeared to over five hundred brethren at one time. What His disciples experienced was not some psychic phenomenon, nor the hallucination of hysteria. The resurrection was not an invention of blind faith, it was the ultimate reality, and it is the cornerstone upon which the whole fabric of Christianity rests.

The Lord gave to His disciples the three-fold evidences of eye, ear, and touch. They saw Him repeatedly in all sorts of settings, including all the old familiar places where they had met and ministered in His earthly ministry. They heard Him explain the meaning of all the Old Testament as it referred to Him in the law, the prophets, the psalms, and throughout the entire Scriptures. They touched Him at His invitation, handling Him and seeing He had flesh and bones, as no mere spirit would have. They saw Him eat, and they joined Him in breakfast by the sea. No wonder John would write in his first Epistle, "That which we have heard, which we have seen with our eyes, which we have gazed upon, and our hands have handled, declare we unto you…" The glory of His transfigured body which only the favored three had seen upon the Holy Mount, was now seen by the many, including five hundred brothers at one time.

Just how important was it for the Lord Jesus to "show Himself alive with many infallible proofs"? If He had not done this, no doubt Christianity would have disappeared long ago. For a while it might have survived as a Jewish sect, or it might have been taken over by the Gnostics as another Greek mythological quasi-religion. But a life-changing, world-turning-upside-down force that transformed an empire and is still changing lives and cultures today? Hardly! Apart from the resurrection of our Lord, the real bodily demonstrable resurrection, we would have no hope, our preaching would be in vain, your faith would be in vain, and we would be of all people the most pitiable. Thank God our Lord took great care to give hardy substance to the words, "He is risen, He is risen indeed."

HE RE-EMPHASIZED THE NEED AND NATURE OF THE HOLY SPIRIT'S WORK

One of His first acts when He appeared to the disciples in their hide-away the evening of His resurrection was to breathe on them and say, "Receive the Holy Spirit. As the Father has sent Me, so send I you." This was not the actual moment of the descent of the Holy Spirit, but it was a prophetic symbol of what would happen on the day of Pentecost.

The conferring of the Spirit was absolutely necessary for them to carry out the commission of Christ to take the Gospel to the ends of the earth. This is why the risen Lord commanded His disciples to tarry in Jerusalem until the promise of the Spirit was fulfilled. It was also necessary for them so the promise of His presence and power as they did His work would be a reality. The baptism of the Spirit and the resulting fullness would be in likeness to their Lord's at His baptism, when the Spirit descended upon Him in the form of a dove and He began His public ministry in the power of the Spirit.

HE TAUGHT THEM FORGIVENESS AND RESTORATION OF THE FALLEN BELIEVER

Christ's dealings with Simon Peter who had denied Him was one of the great lessons which for the most part we have failed to learn. This restoration began when we read these words of the Risen Jesus to the women who were the first at the empty tomb. "Go tell My disciples and Peter that He is going before you into Galilee; there you will see him." Later of course we find the meeting between Peter and Jesus as recorded in John 21, in which Jesus formally forgave and re-installed Peter in the presence of the other disciples. This serves as a beautiful example and a clear pattern for believers when they fall.

HE TAUGHT THEM THE THINGS CONCERNING THE KINGDOM

In many ways, the Lord Jesus had been preparing His disciples for the work and spread of the kingdom beyond the narrow confines of Palestine and Judaism. He had purposely gone through Samaria that He might find one of His lost sheep by a well near Sychar, and through her touch the hearts of hundreds. In His one journey beyond the ancient boundaries of Israel, He encountered a Canaanite woman with a sick child. At her repeated request He healed her child and said to her she had great faith, while earlier He had rebuked His disciples for their little faith. When a Roman centurion in Capernaum sent for Jesus to come and heal his servant who was at the point of death, Jesus said of Him, "I have not found such great faith, even in Israel."

After His resurrection He called His disciples to come to Galilee and there He told them in no uncertain terms the kingdom was to be proclaimed to all the nations of the world, and that these nations should be discipled into keepers of His holy kingdom laws as well as being evangelized. By this great commission He was declaring that the promises God made to Abraham included vastly more than possession of tiny Palestine, and indeed the Promised Land was now extended to the whole world. And the promise in Genesis 22 that through Abraham and his seed all the nations of the earth would be blessed became the mandate and the promise given to the new Israel of God, the church.

The church must always remember that failure to understand and practice this commission is rebellion against the King of the kingdom. Even after the Lord ascended into heaven, He still remains with His church, by His word and Spirit, and by the visible sacraments He ordained.

My challenge to you, beloved is that you begin to more diligently study and glory in the Gospel of the forty day. I believe in doing this we will catch something of the excitement and the Holy Spirit power that gripped those early disciples and made them world changers ready to take the Gospel to the ends of the earth.

I pray God that all of us will be as transformed in our faith as were those believers of old and, like them, become agents of such transformation that a great revival, so sorely needed could, by God's grace, break out in the Church that would astonish and encourage the whole body of Christ world-wide. O how desperately we need such a mighty moving of God's Spirit. May we experience that fresh filling of the Holy Spirit so that we will receive the power promised and readily available to us even as we come together in times of worship, and even more as we leave those blessed places and live for the risen Christ in a world that so desperately needs to know our Christ and enter His kingdom.

For Discussion and Reflection

1. Read again the definition of the doctrine of substitutionary atonement, and then restate it in your own words.

2. Outline the proofs that Jesus gave of His resurrection. Why is the fact of the Resurrection necessary to Christianity?

3. What are the five post-Resurrection teachings of Jesus that comprise the core doctrines of Christianity?

4. Why was the Great Commission (John 20:21-23, Matt. 28:16-20) necessary after Jesus' resurrection? Why is it necessary that we continue to live out that commission today?

4

The Emmaus Road

~

LUKE 24:13-44

In this passage from Luke we read the story of two downcast men who were walking back home to Emmaus that day so very long ago. Little did they know in the darkness of their grief and disillusionment that this would turn out to be the most glorious day of their lives. But that would be only after their amazing experience with the risen Christ along that lonely road. Before that transforming experience they had reached the end of the rope, and the bottom of the pit. Life had lost all meaning and even the faintest expression of joy and peace. Life can be that way. Tragedy spares no one. Many of you have walked that road, and maybe you're still on it. Several years ago, I came back from a brief visit out of town to find that there had been one death and several serious life threatening illnesses in our congregations I was then serving. For each person involved it was a major tragedy.

That same week I heard that Dr James Boice, beloved pastor of Tenth Presbyterian in Philadelphia and one of the leading Reformed Scholars in the world, was discovered to have advanced liver cancer, with only a few days to live. One can only imagine what shock and grief his family, congregation, and close friends must have gone through at that time. No doubt some must have wondered, "Why a man like Dr Boice?" Who could possibly take his place in the Reformed and Presbyterian worlds? Truly during that one traumatic week, it was a time when "sorrows like sea billows roll."

The stories of the lonely and heart-breaking journeys on life's Emmaus roads are many. I dare say each one of us here today could write our own chapters with the ink of tears and the pen of pain. Come with me now and let's join these two as they walk, for another is rapidly catching up with them; so let's consider their grief and ours before that stranger gets too close.

I. THE TWO DISCIPLES BEFORE THE MYSTERIOUS STRANGER JOINED THEIR WALK

We really don't have to wonder about their conversation or even about their feelings of loss and despair. They were pouring that out to each other as they walked, and neither had any word of comfort for the other. Sometimes we tend to forget what life was like before we met the living Lord Jesus, and sometimes we act as if we have never met Him.

Here were two men with broken dreams and shattered hopes. They had believed that Jesus of Nazareth was the true and long awaited Messiah. Their understanding of what that would mean went something like this: even as David had defeated and driven out the hated Philistines and made Israel a great nation, so the heir of David would defeat and drive out the hated Romans and build a kingdom vastly larger and greater than David or Solomon's empire. This Kingdom would be world-wide with Jerusalem the capital city. Sometimes, especially early in our Christian walk, we tend to think, "Now that I've become a Christian, surely my life will be one of joy and happiness," only to discover life in this fallen world may still be filled with tribulation and sorrow.

THE EMMAUS ROAD

They either did not understand what Jesus himself had taught, or else they just didn't listen. At any rate when the Romans put Jesus to death, their world and their dreams collapsed. Everything they believed fell crashing in around them, and life lost its meaning and its hope.

But most people live with broken dreams. How many, many people have come to me and other counselors with their dreams shattered and their hearts broken. Part of the reason is that old myths die hard. Remember this one? "They married and lived happily ever after." Or how about this one: "As soon as I reach my financial goals, I'll be content and happy." Or, "I know my children are good kids and will never disappoint me."

The two Emmaus men seem to think that somehow God had lost control, and nothing really worked out. The silly tales some of the women were telling about angels saying He was alive were more than they could believe.

When the stranger finally caught up with them and began to inquire about their sad countenance and their woeful conversation, they poured out their lament about the death of Jesus and added, "But we had hoped that He was going to be the One who would deliver Israel." So far as they knew, their hopes had been destroyed, and now they are turning their backs on those hopes and leaving them in the blood and dust of Golgotha.

How many times I have heard a similar lament, "I tried religion and it just didn't work." Guess what? "Religion" has never worked, and the living God refuses to be "worked" by fallible self-centered people. Maybe you are on that Emmaus Road right now; disillusioned, confused, and disappointed with life and thinking to yourself, "But I had hoped He would have protected me."

The mysterious stranger finally caught up with the men, and the same thing which happened to them could happen to you. This could be your Emmaus Road experience with the Lord Jesus.

II. WHAT JESUS SHOWED THEM ON THAT ROAD

We know that the mysterious stranger was the risen Christ with power to reveal himself or withhold recognition. They did not know who He was, but as He questioned them they poured out their misery and their woes. He listened, He understood, but the most important thing was He rebuked their unbelief and their failure to understand all He had taught them those wonderful three years of His earthly ministry.

And just what did Jesus tell these men? First, He told them what had happened to the Christ had long since been foretold, and was an exact fulfillment of God's plan. Nothing had gone amiss, but had worked out just the way God had ordained from before the foundation of the world. Then during that seven mile walk He simply explained the full meaning of the Bible to them. He showed them the only way to understand Scripture was to see all of it as being focused on Christ. God was still very much in control, ruling and overruling everything that had happened during those last days of Jesus' life to make everything come out just right, and just as the Old Testament Scriptures had foretold.

You want an answer to your doubts and confusion? You want healing for your hurting heart? Believe it or not the answer lies right in your hands in the pages of that familiar old book we call the Bible. But you have to read it with understanding and a searching heart, a believing mind, and surrendered will. Look for Jesus on every page, seek to see and know Him beyond and within the written word. Beg Him to abide with you, for your day is far spent.

Ask Him to be the permanent guest in the inner room of your life. He will come in and abide with you forever. Don't trust your own wisdom, don't look for some mystic experience; simply trust His word and feast on the wonders of His truth. And as He breaks the bread of life to you, He will reveal himself in a true, living, and life-changing way. Grace, mercy, and peace will flood your soul, and even as you see your earthly dreams and longings fade away, He will give you true riches. When life has lost its taste, He will feed you on the true manna. For He is the risen living Lord.

III. THE TWO DISCIPLES AFTER THEIR EXPERIENCE WITH THE LORD

When the word tells us that their eyes were opened so that they knew Jesus as the risen, reigning Lord, God is offering to us the same glorious experience. The word had truly become alive to them for the first time. Their hearts were aflame with joy, wonder, and zeal. "Did not our heart burn within us while talked with us on the road, and while He opened the Scriptures to us," they said. Oh how I long for this to be your experience in God's house every Lord's Day and every time we open the word, being illumined by the Holy Spirit.

These two men of old were not the last to discover such things. John Wesley had been a preacher and a missionary for years before he found the Lord in a personal encounter in a prayer meeting. "Then and there," he testified, "my heart was strangely warmed." John Calvin wanted a personal symbol to display for all to see what had happened in his life. He chose this symbol, a burning heart held out to the Lord in an open hand, with these words, "My heart I give thee Lord, eagerly, sincerely." This grew out of great struggle to obey God's call knowing it might well cost him his life and all earthly joys. John Knox studied under Calvin for three years, then returned to Scotland with his heart aflame with love for Christ and His word, and as he struggled to win that sin-darkened nation for Christ, he cried out to the Lord, "O God give me Scotland, or I shall die."

IV. THE JOYFUL JOURNEY BACK FROM EMMAUS

Though the day was far spent, back they sped to the city to tell the others of what had happened on the Emmaus road.

That's always the way it is. When the Lord Jesus finds you and brings you to Himself, and redeems your life, someone is going to hear about it, and many empty, heart-broken people need to hear it from you. The news we bear is the Good News, the glorious news that Christ died for our sins according to the Scriptures, that He was buried, and that He arose again the third day according to Scripture.

We may still have roads to walk that will lead us through the shadows of pain and grief. But never again will we walk them alone, for He, the risen Lord, during His earthly life was tempted and tried in all points as we are. He knew all the bitter disappointments you have known. He even knew the grief of feeling utterly abandoned by the Father, for when He took our sins upon Himself, He was. So He walks beside us on our Emmaus road, but not just to share our woes and sorrows, but to lift us up, and give to us joy and hope that will be our strength until we see Him face to face. "Face to face with Christ my Savior, face to face what will it be, when in rapture I behold Him, Jesus Christ who died for me." And consider this, O best beloved, we shall also see each other face to face and our joy will be complete.

For Discussion and Reflection

1. Why do you think the two disciples did not recognize Jesus when they first met Him along the road? What helps you recognize that it is Jesus who is walking beside you when you are in the midst of struggles?

2. When did the two disciples finally recognize Jesus? What is the significance of the action that sparked their awareness of His identity?

3. If Jesus were to take a walk with you today, what would you want to talk about with Him?

4. In this chapter, we read that Jesus "showed them the only way to understand Scripture was to see all of it as being focused on Christ." Does this change your view of the Old Testament or of Scripture as a whole? If so, how? Is there a cost to losing the message that all of Scripture is ultimately about Jesus?

5

Unforgettable Encounter

∼

LUKE 24:28-52

When we recite "The Apostles Creed" we say of our Lord Jesus, "...On the third day He arose again from the dead, He ascended into heaven, and sitteth at the right hand of God the Father Almighty." All of which we very joyfully say and fervently believe, but the truth of the matter is, we leave out a very important truth, which is found in these words from Acts: "To whom (the disciples) He presented Himself alive after His passion, by many infallible proofs, being seen by them during forty days, and speaking of things pertaining to the kingdom of God."

I will be showing you from Scripture what these things are and what they mean to us. And it starts with the first of these forty days, late in the evening of the first day, Easter Sunday.

Luke has just been telling us about two disciples who had an amazing encounter with the risen Lord as they walked from Jerusalem to the little village of Emmaus, where they presumably lived. A lot has been written and said about that Emmaus walk long ago, but not so much about what followed when these same two disciples hurried back to Jerusalem to share their joy with the others who were huddled fearfully in a hidden room somewhere in the city. We get the idea from reading John's account of this same incident that the doors were shut, locked, and barricaded for fear of the Jews and what they might try to do to these disciples of Jesus.

The two from Emmaus obviously knew where the others were hiding, and so went straight there to tell of their incredible encounter with the Lord. But before they could tell their wondrous tale, they were greeted with these words, "The Lord is risen indeed and has appeared unto Simon." Then they began to relate what had happened to them on the road and how the Lord had revealed Himself at their evening meal. Can't you just sense the excitement and hear the many voices as they spoke and interrupted one another, as each one wanted to tell his part of the story?

Suddenly in the midst of their excited babbling, Jesus was there, right among them. The doors were shut and locked, no one had seen Him enter, but He was there, speaking the old familiar greeting which from now on would have a new and glorious richness and meaning: "Shalom," which we translate, "Peace to you." But at the moment, the greeting of peace terrified them and frightened them out of their wits! They thought they were seeing a ghost.

There is almost a note of humor in the whole thing, and certainly there must have been a twinkle in His eye, and a broad smile as the Lord quieted their fears and revealed Himself wonderfully alive. What a moment! What an experience! Don't you wish you could have been there at just that time? But you may receive the same three wonderful gifts He gave them there. For what He gave his disciples in that upper room on Easter evening, He also gives to you, and if you will accept these gifts, you will discover they are precious and wonderful above any gift.

What are these priceless pearls?

I. CHRIST GAVE THEM THE GIFT OF ASSURANCE

I would suggest to you that if you could just be sure that Christ really did rise from the dead, that He is alive at the Father's right hand praying for you, and that He is coming again in power and glory to judge and rule the earth, your life would be filled with peace, joy, hope, and the deepest possible meaning.

These men and women had all believed everything He had taught them. They had been crushed by His suffering and death on the cross. They were confused, frightened, and uncertain about Him and themselves. Some, like Mary, and even Peter and John, claimed to have seen and spoken with Him. The two from Emmaus certainly had walked and talked with Him, but still it was all so strange and even unreal. Now Jesus came to them, right there in the room. He hadn't entered by the door, it was locked and barred. But He was there so they simply assumed He was just a spirit, a ghost.

So Jesus offered them a four-fold proof that He was really and fully alive. "Why are you frightened, and why do you doubt? Look at my hands and feet." Obviously the nail marks of His crucifixion were still very visible. Then He invited them to confirm what their eyes could see by saying, "Handle me and see, a spirit does not have flesh and bones as you see I have." So powerful was that experience that fifty or more years later when John wrote his short little letter we call I John, he still remembered touching the risen Christ that night and said of Him, "That which we have seen and heard and handled, we declare unto you."

Once more Jesus reached out His hands and showed them His lacerated feet, but still they did not fully believe for joy and wonder. They were thinking, "It's just too good to be true!" And some of you may even be thinking the same right now. The Lord then offered the final touch. "Do you have any food?"(Who ever heard of a ghost being hungry?) Right there, in front of them all He began to eat what they had been eating, fish and some honeycomb. When you enter His house to worship, He is there by His word and Holy Spirit. He meets us at His table and through a simple symbolic meal reminds us of that post-resurrection meal, and the coming one He will once again eat with us in the Father's kingdom.

Will you accept His proofs? Will you share the joy of the Emmaus two, and the others who met that night so long ago? Will you hear the Lord's holy humor as He says, "Why are you so fearful and why do you doubt?" A mere ghost doesn't have a resurrected, real human body. A ghost can't eat fish and honey. He offers you assurance. Will you accept it from His nail scarred hand?

II. HE GAVE THEM A CLEAR UNDERSTANDING Of WHAT THE BIBLE REALLY MEANS

He reminded them of His previous teaching, before His death on the cross. "...that all things must be fulfilled which were written in the law of Moses, the Prophets, and the Psalms concerning Me." By these words, Moses, Prophets, and Psalms, He was saying that the whole Old Testament bore witness to His life, His teachings, His death, and His resurrection. This is how to understand the Bible, all of it. Then the Lord "opened their understanding that they might comprehend the Scriptures." What He did for Clopas and the other disciple on the Emmaus road, He now did for the whole assembly of disciples. Dr G. Campbell Morgan said of this verse "He disentangled" their minds. In fact the Greek word used almost sounds like "disentangle," and it means to completely open up and make very clear.

It is almost as if He gave them a whole new Bible, so far as their understanding was concerned. When it begins to dawn on us that the whole Bible, from Genesis through Revelation, is really about Jesus Christ, it gives us a whole new outlook and eagerness to discover our Lord on every page, in every prophecy, precept, and poetry. I will never forget the testimony of a once very liberal Presbyterian preacher who became a believer years ago. He said of his own experience, "I began to read the Bible as if it were all true, and one day I realized that it was, and my life and ministry has been transformed."

One may almost imagine these men and women later trying to convince their kinsmen and other Jewish friends who knew the content of the Old Testament just as well as they did. "Don't you see, can't you understand? It all makes sense when you see it as a testimony to Jesus, the Messiah." Let me add this; any teaching or preaching of the Bible that does not present Christ as the heart and soul of the message is off-base.

III. FINALLY HE GAVE THEM A GREAT PROMISE AND A GREAT TASK

The message is clear. Christ suffered and died, and was raised again, so that repentance and remission of sin should be preached in His name to all nations. Certainly it is a message of love. But that message of love must include at its very core, repentance and remission of sin, or it lacks the depth and the convincing power of the Holy Spirit to truly change lives.

They were eye witnesses to the great truth of Christ and His salvation. Their eye witness has been passed on to us, and we have learned by real and glorious personal experience that the message is true. Now we are heart witnesses to these same wonderful truths: Christ, in His birth, life, teaching, death, and resurrection fulfills the revelation of God's plan of salvation. This now is our message, and our task is to make this known.

The Promise? That we will be filled with the power of the Holy Spirit as we are faithful to our task. Jesus Christ makes this solemn promise to you. "You will be endued with power from on high."

Get serious about being a witness, and you will receive power. Without that heaven-sent power we are spiritually impotent, but with it we may become, and indeed must and will become, world changers.

For Discussion and Reflection

1. Why were the doors to the upper room locked and the disciples in hiding? Why were they afraid when Jesus appeared in the room? What do these things say about their state of mind and about their faith? What does Jesus do to calm their fears?

2. What are the three gifts that Jesus gave His disciples on Easter evening? With such gifts, why do we doubt?

3. Reflecting back on the quote from the Presbyterian preacher, have you experienced a life transformation as a result of Bible study? How did your transformation occur? What does it look like?

4. Reflecting upon Jesus' words in Luke 24:44-49 in light of what the disciples had been through over the previous few days, what thoughts and feelings do you imagine they experienced in response to His charge to be "world changers"? How do you imagine they responded at first? What is your response to this charge? How can you be - or how are you being - a world changer for Christ in your corner of the world?

6

Celebrating the Ascension of Christ

~

ACTS 2:29-36

Strangely enough, I have never heard one person ask another, "What did you get for Ascension?" Nor have I heard any one compliment another saying, "What a lovely new Ascension outfit you have on!"

Yet when we meet for worship on Ascension Sunday, we stand and confess Christ in these words, "He was conceived by the Holy Ghost, born of the virgin Mary, suffered under Pontius Pilate, was crucified, dead and buried, He descended into hell. The third day He rose again from the dead, He ascended into heaven and sitteth on the right hand of God the Father Almighty, etc. It is the last two of these affirmations which give validity to the others, and paves the way for confessing, "From thence He shall come to judge the living and the dead."

Christ's bodily ascension into heaven and taking His seat of power and authority at God's right hand are really part of one grand event, the enthronement of Christ Jesus as King of kings and Lord of lords. What are the issues here, and why is the ascension so important? It boils down to this. Is Jesus Christ alive today? If so where and in what form? If He is not alive in the true and real sense of the word, then Christianity is either just an empty ideal, or an escapism from reality, or even a huge fraud. The majority of the media, the liberal educational establishment, and most certainly the icons of Hollywood would all have you believe the latter and are at work night and day in their attempt to convince you that Christ was a mere man, very much like the rest of us, and that the whole basis and structure of Christianity is a deliberate fraud.

On the other hand if He is alive, and if the accounts of His ascension are true, then we live in a hope that will not be denied, and the best is yet to be. First let's look at the facts as presented, and then at the meaning of these events for now and for the future.

THE ASCENSION AND ENTHRONEMENT OF JESUS TO THE FATHER'S RIGHT HAND AS EVENTS CLOSELY RELATED TO THE RESURRECTION

The reports of the ascension as given in the Gospels and the book of Acts, are presented in very much the same way all other events associated with the birth, life, death, and resurrection of the Lord Jesus are given us. It was a historical event which happened before the same eye witnesses who saw Him after His resurrection. After Jesus had finished His forty days of ministry to the disciples following His resurrection, He led them outside the city of Jerusalem and gave them His final instructions. Then while they were looking on He began to be lifted up before their eyes until a cloud received Him out of their sight. He left the realm of time and entered the realm of eternity. He left one place, earth, and entered into another, heaven.

As the disciples were gazing up into heaven in awe-struck wonder, two angelic messengers suddenly appeared and assured them that this same Jesus, who you see being taken up from you into heaven, will so come again in like manner in the same way they saw Him go into heaven.

THE SIGNIFICANCE OF CHRIST'S ENTHRONEMENT AT THE FATHER'S RIGHT HAND

"He ascended into heaven, and sitteth at the right hand of God the Father Almighty." This is a position of power and honor, and does not imply He is at rest, with nothing more to do. It indicates the completion of one great undertaking and the beginning of another, equally as great. Calvin said the accession of Christ to God's right hand means that He received the reins of government of both heaven and earth, and from that time forth, heaven and earth are constituted under the same rule and Ruler. This, said Calvin, is the confirmation of His announcement to the disciples after His resurrection, that "All power in heaven and on earth has been given to Him."

To reinforce the concept of an ongoing ministry by the Risen Christ, the new Testament speaks of Him as "standing at God's right hand," "walking among the seven golden lamp stands, which are the church," waging unrelenting warfare against Satan and all spiritual wickedness. "He is not dead nor doth He sleep." The Lord Jesus, from His throne of glory, is powerfully at work in your behalf, and because He is you will persevere to the end and be saved.

THE MINISTRY OF THE ASCENDED CHRIST

There are many ways of expressing this ongoing ministry, but perhaps the best way is found in the words of the Westminster Shorter Catechism when it asks, "What offices does Christ execute as our Redeemer?" The answer is classic and very biblical, "Christ as our redeemer, executes the offices of a Prophet, of a Priest, and of a King, both in His estate of humiliation and exaltation." Let's look at His present ministry under these headings.

AS A PROPHET

Christ came to earth as the mighty prophet Moses had predicted would one day come. He was a prophet who proclaimed God's word, and was in Himself God's word. But that was during His earthly ministry, what about now in His heavenly estate and ministry? The enthroned Lord of glory continues His work as God's Prophet by the Holy Spirit, whom He sent from heaven. It was by the Holy Spirit the apostles received and wrote down the word of God, showing to us the things of Christ, and explaining their meaning. Furthermore it is the same Spirit who enlightens our minds to comprehend this written word, and who enables us to obey it, though imperfectly. The Holy Spirit whom the Lord Jesus sends to us from the Father is the one who enables the faithful preaching of that holy word. Christ continues to supply the Spirit that the church might be able to proclaim His word, and in these ways continues to execute His office as a prophet.

AS A PRIEST

When Christ had finished His earthly ministry, especially His atoning death on the cross, He took once more His rightful place of power and glory at God's right hand. He entered the real Holiest of Holies as the perfect High Priest, after the order of Melchizedek, and brought before the Father the once and for all perfect sacrifice for sins. For He was both the Priest and the Lamb of God who takes away the sin of the world. At His death on the cross, the veil of the temple was rent from top to bottom, and God and sinner reconciled. His priestly work, like that of the earthly priests of old, included making intercession for His people. So from heaven's high throne of glory, He, the Lord Jesus, intercedes for us. He was tempted and tried in all points as we are, yet without sin. So he is a merciful and faithful high Priest, who is touched with the feelings of our infirmities, yet with sinless power which enables us to know that He will in the end triumph for us and in us.

He who intercedes for us is the Father's beloved Son to whom He will grant every request. Jesus said of us while praying with His disciples as recorded in John 17, "Father it is my desire that all you have given Me may be with Me that they may behold My glory."

His work as High Priest assures us of our continuance and growth in grace (both are needed!). His work as High Priest also is the foundation for the priesthood of all believers, as we join Him in making intercession for the saints according to the will of God.

AS KING

Christ by nature and the Father's appointment is a King. From His throne of glory He remains the head of the church, which is His body. He rules the church by His word and Spirit, and through His appointed officers. But He never surrenders that rule into their hands in and of themselves, but only as they are true to the Word, and faithful to the appointed tasks. He also is the King of each member of His body, the church. He deserves the allegiance and loyalty of those whom he has redeemed from sin and death. The now invisible King on His invisible throne is no less a King than when He shall return in visible power and glory. To be your King then, He must be your King now.

As the king in one of the parables He told, He has gone into a far country and has entrusted His kingdom to faithful servants who will be true to Him and watch unceasingly for His return.

As Christians we confess Jesus Christ as the living Lord. For us there is no other Name under heaven given among men whereby we must be saved. Because He is truly alive and at the Father's right hand, we have the blessed hope that He will come again and claim the kingdom before all creatures, who will bend the knees and confess that He is Lord to the glory of God the Father.

Some will confess this to their everlasting shame and regret, others with joy and vindication.

Said one of the puritans of old, "I looked into my own heart and saw naught but darkness, sin, and pride. I looked to the living Christ and found a prophet whose wisdom could dispel my darkness, a priest who could take away my sin, and a king who could subdue my stubborn will and take me into His kingdom. 'Tis good we met."

For Discussion and Reflection

1. This chapter discusses the idea of "an ongoing ministry by the Risen Christ." Have you ever thought of the ascended Christ as continuing the ministry that he started during His time on earth? Reflect again on this chapter, as well as on Acts 2:29-36. Jot down what these sources tell us about how He continues to move and work in the world from His exalted state.

2. In Acts 2:29-36, Peter sets out to prove that the Lord spoken of in Old Testament prophecies - specifically noting David's prophecy - is indeed Jesus Christ, the resurrected One. What proofs does Peter give that this is the truth?

3. As you live your life as a disciple of Jesus, what is the significance that we worship a living King and not a dead prophet?

4. "... He has gone into a far country and has entrusted His Kingdom to faithful servants who will be true to Him ..." How do you honor this commission of stewardship? How do you work in your own life to preserve and grow the Kingdom of God? How do you see your own congregation - your "branch" of the Body of Christ - striving to honor the work He has entrusted to us?

7

The Lamb Upon the Throne

∼

ACTS 1:1-11

In one of the most touching and beautiful scenes in all literature, Alfred Lord Tennyson describes the death and passing of King Arthur. His body is lovingly placed on a funeral barge, and Sir Bedivere his true friend stands watching the barge as it recedes across the waters. Then there comes to his ears from far across the waters, faint and far off as from beyond the limits of the world:

> *"Sounds as if some fair city were one voice, around a King returning from His wars."*

There lived once a King far more noble and pure hearted than Arthur. One who battled the enemies of His people, defending them from the most deadly and powerful foe. One who gave His life a ransom for many and died to set the prisoners free. His heart-broken subjects could scarcely believe their own senses when three days after His death in battle, He appeared to them alive again, triumphant and victorious.

When the awe-stricken disciples watched in wonder, on that day of His ascension back to the Father, the Lord Jesus said His parting words to them and then began to ascend before their very eyes, until a cloud received Him out of their sight. If only they had ears to hear, they would have heard far more than Sir Bedivere heard as the body of Arthur passed over the mist-shrouded water. Indeed they would have heard a thunderous, joyful celebration as all heaven with its redeemed saints and glorious angels welcomed their King returning victorious from His wars.

Forty days after the Lord Jesus began to show Himself alive after His crucifixion, He went back to heaven to begin His invisible reign, and to prepare for His return in power and glory when the reign will be visible, powerful and glorious.

I. THE NEGLECTED ARTICLE OF FAITH

While it is true that all liturgical churches have the Ascension on their church year calendars for observation and celebration, many people have paid scant attention to this grand event, and probably some have never heard of it. It is never celebrated by the general public as both Christmas and Easter are, and seldom celebrated even in biblical churches. For the believer it is just as important as either Christmas or Easter, and neither is complete without the ascension of the Lord Jesus back to heaven after finishing His work on earth. Though ignored by most of this generation of believers, historically this doctrine has played an important role in supporting and sustaining believers through dark and bloody days.

When Stephen was on trial for his life and witness, it was apparent that his enemies were determined to silence him by death. But boldly Stephen accused them of being guilty of the death of the Messiah. When they heard this they were cut to the heart and gnashed their teeth at him. But he being filled with the Holy Spirit gazed into heaven and saw the glory of God, and Jesus standing at God's right hand. "Look," he said, "I see heavens opened and the Son of Man standing at God's right hand." Then they stopped their ears and laid hands on him and dragged him out of the city and stoned him to death. But even in dying he still looked to the ascended Lord, saying, "Lord Jesus, receive my spirit." And then, "Lord do not charge them with this sin."

Shortly thereafter, the man who held the coats of those who killed Stephen, Saul of Tarsus, was on his way to Damascus to have more Christians put to death, when a great light blinded him, and a voice from heaven called him by name. It was again the ascended Christ. The same Lord Jesus, who received the spirit of dying Stephen, claimed one of his murderers for the kingdom and transformed him into Paul the Apostle. So down through the long history of the church we have celebrated and rejoiced in the knowledge that our Lord Jesus is at the Father's right hand praying for us and awaiting the Father's command to return to the earth and rescue His people and take them to their eternal home.

During the dreadful days of the counter reformation when believers by the tens of thousands were being persecuted for the sake of Lord Jesus and His crown rights as the only true Head and Lord of the Church, it was the preaching of the ascension which gave them courage to face the fire and sword of persecution and death. Our bold Scottish forebears believed that neither the king nor the pope in Rome should usurp the crown rights of King Jesus, for He had ascended far above all principalities and powers. For this confident faith, they died as martyrs for their true Lord.

But what is the ascension, what does it mean, and why is it so important for believers?

II. THE GRAND EVENT

The return of the Lord Jesus to heaven is told in simple, straightforward language by Luke, both in his Gospel and the book of Acts. Forty days after the Lord's resurrection from the dead, He met with His disciples on Mt Olive, and after His final instructions and promise, He was taken up in the air, until a cloud received Him out of their sight. He left one place, earth, and entered another, heaven. He left one realm, time, and entered into another, eternity. The book of Hebrews tells us that He went into the very presence of God the Father, and there began His work of intercession for you and me.

The Bible teaches us that there is a central place of God's presence and power in this vast universe. Many of the modern concepts of the physical universe substantiate the idea of a central, vital hub or core of the universe.

Christ in His glorified human body passed from the realm of time and space into the greater realm of eternity. He entered another dimension, unknown to human experience, but long sensed and sought. As the amazed and baffled disciples looked on, still gazing into the now empty sky, they were assured that this same Jesus, whom they had seen ascending to heaven, would come again in like manner one day. No doubt they were dismayed, for little did they know that all heaven was about to break loose on the earth with the coming of the Holy Spirit.

III. THE GLORIOUS MEANING AND ACCOMPLISHMENTS OF THE ASCENSION

1. For Christ:
The ascension was the completion of His earthly work. He took His rightful place, presented the perfect and final sacrifice for sin, and began His reign as King and High Priest. When Jesus went back to heaven, He went home, and there's always something special about going back home again. A few years ago, I preached a revival series near the town where I grew up. There was something very special about going back home and seeing family and old friends. That's just a tiny and imperfect illustration of what our Lord experienced when He returned to His home. Now He would converse not only with Moses and

Elijah as He had on the Mount of Transfiguration, but with all the redeemed saints who are in heaven because their Lord and Savior came down to earth to win their salvation by His perfect obedience and His atoning death.

2. For us:
   A. The ascension means we have an advocate with the Father, One who was tempted and tried in all points as we are, yet without sin; a merciful and faithful High Priest who is touched with the feelings of our infirmities. Because He is there, not just in Spirit form, but also in human flesh of the resurrected body, there is a special bond between earth and heaven, and between believers on earth and believers in heaven, and Christ is that bond.

   B. He became the head of a new race of people, the second Adam, as Paul described Him; and by the new birth, we are born into that new race of humanity. He was the bold pioneer, who opened a closed realm for all His followers.

   After the completion of the treaty with France, called the Louisiana Purchase, which transferred vast regions of an unexplored continent to the new nation, President Jefferson called upon two bold young men to go into that uncharted wilderness in preparation for the multitudes which would one day follow them and make their homes there. Lewis and Clark fulfilled their obligation by bravely facing the perils and hardships of the unknown. So the Lord Jesus became the bold Pioneer who opened heaven for us that we might live there for all eternity.

   C. By the ascension, the Holy Spirit was released to come into the world in a new and powerful way. By His mighty presence, the new birth is now possible; the mind and will of God is made known through Holy Scripture, and you have a comforter, a helper, and a guide.

D. The ascension was a sign and testimony of His return. "This same Jesus will so come in like manner as you have seen Him leave." His return will be a visible, personal, victorious, and glorious return which every eye shall see, and every ear shall hear. So much for a "secret return" as taught by some sects, and believed by multitudes of gullible believers who would rather read popular "end time" novels than seriously study the Scriptures.

Conclusions:

In olden times, when the king of the realm was in residence in his castle and among his people, he would fly his personal banner from the highest rampart of his castle. It was a sign that his people were safely under his protection, and that he was available to hear their pleas. But when he went off to war, he took his banner into battle with him. Then there was sadness and fear lest an enemy should invade and ravage the people. But after the king returned from his wars, once more the banner would be seen far and near which proclaimed the king is in his castle, all is well, his people are safe once more.

So from the tallest pinnacle of heaven, a banner is flying. It is the banner of Christ our King, victorious in His wars, and on His throne, and available to His people, now and forever. There that banner will fly until the day He goes forth to His final battle, conquering and to conquer. This is what we celebrate today, and this is what we mean when we say, He ascended into heaven and sitteth at the right hand of God the Father Almighty. Our King is on His throne. He rules and defends His church by the Word and Holy Spirit. He awaits only the word of the Father, and then what is now seen by faith will be seen by sight. What is longed for, prayed for, yearned for will give way to a reality far more glorious than mind can conceive. So rejoice believers. Behold His banner of love and grace is flying from the highest ramparts of heaven. May it also fly from the tall steeple of this church, and even more from the hearts of us all, as our testimony that we are His people. Our loved ones in Christ are safely there waiting for the grand reunion we all long for. The ascension is God's pledge that all the blessed promises yet to be fulfilled will most certainly come to fruition when our Lord returns. What more can He say, than to you He hath said!

For Discussion and Reflection

1. Just as it was important for the disciples to see Jesus taken up into heaven, how is the knowledge of the Ascension significant to us as Christians today? If Jesus had not ascended, what would that have meant for Him and for us?

2. How do you think the followers of Jesus were affected by the promise that He would return? How are you affected by that promise?

3. What does the Ascension mean in terms of the completion of Jesus' ministry?

4. In the Apostles' Creed, what is meant by "He ascended into heaven and sitteth at the right hand of God the Father Almighty"?

8

Salvaging a Fallen Saint

~

JOHN 21

What do you do when you realize that you have really "blown it"? How do you handle it when you've gone on record as being one of Christ's true followers and then in a sudden, unexpected moment when all your defenses are down you have seriously damaged your credibility as a servant of Christ, you have wounded another believer or perhaps even many believers, and worst of all by word and/or deed you have broken your promise to the Lord Jesus; you know you have let Him down and you have behaved in such a way that you have in effect denied Him?

These are not theoretical questions. These are all too frequent occurrences even in the best and strongest Christians...even a Simon Peter. John 21 is often referred to as a sort of postlude to the grand drama of John's Gospel. But without it John's Gospel would be incomplete, and we would be left without answers to one of life's most painful questions: "What hope is there for believers when they deny the Lord and bring serious damage to the body of believers?" How can you endure and overcome that dreadful, terrible feeling when you know you have failed your

Lord, just when you needed to stand strong and true?

How gracious is the Holy Spirit to have John record this touching story of how our wonderful Lord restored His fallen saint both to fellowship and to service in His kingdom. What hope and comfort this story brings. What clear instructions are given to those who know how often we fail, even with our best intentions.

This story really begins in the upper room where Jesus gathered with His disciples on that last night before the cross. He was there to celebrate the Passover for the last time, and to inaugurate the New Covenant Passover, the Lord's Supper. It was there the Lord also began to prepare His disciples for the terrible trial which lay ahead for them, and for His death on the cross. As the evening wore on Jesus made it very clear that He would soon leave them, and all the disciples were filled with consternation and grief.

Then He said, "All of you will leave Me and forsake Me." That was just too much for Simon who was already confused and troubled. "Lord, though all others will forsake you, yet I will never forsake you. I am willing to die for you." He meant that with all his heart and soul. What He didn't count on was that hidden weakness which lies in all of us, and manifests itself at the worst possible moment.

I. JESUS' WARNNG TO PETER, AND HIS PROMISE TO HIM

After Peter's outburst and vehement protest that he would never fail his dear Lord and Master, Jesus clearly warned Peter that he was not as strong as he imagined. Jesus told Peter that he would deny Him three times before the break of the next day. He told him that Satan desired to sift him as wheat. Peter the rock would crumble like sand before the night was over. Can you imagine the hurt of Peter? How could the Lord possibly think that of him, and why would He say it in front of all the others? (Isn't it true that we are more concerned about other people knowing we have sinned than about the act itself?) How very much like Peter we all are!

And even though the Lord knew what Peter did not know about himself and his coming fall, still He also said to Peter, "But I have prayed for you." How gracious! How precious to know that our Lord prays for us even though knowing that we will fail Him time after time. We break His wonderful heart by our sins. He breaks our proud hearts by His kindness and grace. Do you remember the next words that Jesus spoke to Peter and all the others? "Let not your heart be troubled, neither let it be afraid." Have you ever connected the last verse of John 13, with the first verse of John 14?

No Christian ever falls into sin unwarned. God speaks clearly His word of warning both by precept and by example. Why do you think this whole story was recorded? Why would the failure and sin of the great saints of old be paraded before our eyes? And it is not just through the failure of saints of old, but all around us we see what happens when believers are overtaken by sin, and the devastation it brings into their lives and to many others as well. Still, like Simon Peter we say "Not me Lord. Though all others fall and fail, I will never." Dangerous and foolish words beloved!

II. THE TRIAL AND FALL

The trial of his faith and strength came much sooner than Peter could imagine, and in a much different way. When the soldiers came to take away Jesus in the garden, led by the traitor Judas, Peter was quick to respond. "Over my dead body!" he likely yelled as he waded into them, sword flashing. He would show them and Jesus that he meant what he said. He was fearless and willing to die for Jesus' sake. But what's this? Jesus rebuked him saying, "Put away your sword." Then He healed the only man Peter had managed to wound. That was too much. If he couldn't fight, what could he do? He ran. But he was not through yet. He followed from afar and when he saw where Jesus was taken, he slipped into the courtyard, warming himself at the fire of the enemy. The story is too well known to repeat it word for word, but faced with the sneering accusations that he was a follower of Jesus, he denied that accusation three times. The third time, as he was cursing and swearing he did not even know this man called Jesus. Then two things happened almost simultaneously. A rooster was crowing to announce a new day, and Jesus was standing there in his bonds, surrounded by the enemies, and looking at and listening to Peter's words. The next thing that happened was Peter stumbling away into the darkness to weep.

III. NOTE WELL THE PATHWAY TO TREASON

If there is one lesson in all this we must learn, it is to see how we are led step by step into the same path of destruction and ruin.

      A. Pride
      B. Failure to watch and pray
      C. Following Jesus from afar and being warmed at the fires of the enemy

IV. RECOVERY AND RESTORATION

Now move forward a few days. The Lord had died on the cross and was buried. Then He gloriously rose from the dead. He sent this word by the faithful women: "Go tell My disciples and Peter that I have arisen from the grave." Peter was there in the upper room again when Jesus came and stood in their midst. He heard the Lord open the Scriptures of the Old Testament to assure His disciples that all these events were a part of God's glorious plan of salvation. The Lord appeared on several occasions, showing Himself alive with many infallible proofs.

But still there was the undeniable record of Peter's sad and serious fall, just when the Lord needed him most. To this point nothing had been said about it. Peter was still grieving, even while hoping against hope he might be forgiven and restored. Here is how the Lord Jesus worked in his heart to bring about that restoration.

Since Peter had never really dealt with his failure, there was for him only one answer. Just go back to his old life and occupation. Back to the boat and out on the sea he went to pick up the broken pieces of his shattered life. That didn't work either. All night long he and his friends labored with no fish. Then as they came ashore as dawn was breaking there was One standing on the shore, just as he had three years before, and with the same question, and the same direction, and with the same results except for one thing. This time the net was not broken, though the catch was enormous. John cried out, "It is the Lord." Then Peter swam eagerly to shore where Jesus was waiting…with breakfast already prepared, and with the gracious offer of forgiveness and restoration. It was time, the Lord's time for Peter to face his sin, and his Lord. Note the simplicity of Christ's method. Peter had professed a great love and loyalty for Jesus. He had failed. But the Lord knowing both the heart and the failure of Peter confronted Peter with the simple question. "Do you love Me?" (Repeat the conversation, and the call renewed…noting what He did NOT say.) Then came the three-fold charge to feed and shepherd the sheep of Christ after His pattern.

CONCLUSION

Learn how to deal with your sin, and how to deal with brothers and sisters when they sin too. Face the Lord. Face and acknowledge the sin. Repent and be prepared to serve Him. Stop worrying about what other believers might say, think or do. (Lord, what about this man?)
You follow Me.

For Discussion and Reflection

1. Set aside some quiet time to ponder the question posed at the beginning of this chapter. Choose one such situation in your life and write about what happened, how you handled the situation after realizing the hurt you caused, and how you could have better responded to it. Finally, how did that experience guide you in subsequent instances of "really blowing it"? What is your primary weakness in such situations? What can you do to overcome that weakness?

2. Consider the question from the other side. When you are the injured party, how do you respond? Do you struggle with forgiveness? Are you able to extend love and mercy as Jesus did for Peter? If not, what are the weaknesses that hold you back?

3. Why is it important to revisit instances in which we have failed one another - and, in so doing, failed Jesus - and bring the failing before God? Why is it important to our life in Christ that we seek and receive forgiveness? (Think about how Jesus' forgiveness affected Peter.)

4. Re-read John 21:15-17. Each affirmation of love is followed by a command. Describe the difference between love that is not expressed through supporting action versus love that is expressed through deeds.

9

Thomas the Believer

JOHN 20:24-31

Many years ago, in the 1920s, Georgia Tech's football team went through the entire season undefeated, and became one of the first southern teams to be invited to play in the prestigious Rose Bowl on January 1. This team had some outstanding players, and none better than their captain and All-American Roy Riegal. He had led the Tech team through a tough schedule of the best teams in the south, undefeated and untied. Yet he was never remembered for his excellent ability, nor his leadership, nor even that he was a bona-fide All-American player.

When Tech went to the Rose Bowl to play an undefeated California Golden Bears team, not many people thought they could win. But with Roy Riegal's play and determination, they went ahead and dominated a low scoring game. In the final quarter, with Tech leading 8-0, a chance came for them to sew up the game and remain undefeated. The California running back fumbled the ball in his own territory, and after a mad scramble and a confused mele, Riegal came up with the ball and set sail for the California end zone. The crowd went wild as he ran and even the California players seemed unable and even uninterested in trying to tackle him. Finally he was brought down on the two yard line, by one of his own team mates. You see, in the confusion, Roy Riegal, All-American star, had run in the wrong direction. Though he was saved the embarrassment of actually scoring a touchdown for the opposition, two plays later, California scored to come within one point of tying the game. That's how the game ended, Tech 8, California 7; and Tech remained undefeated. And Roy Riegal, the fine young man who had made All-American, and had led Tech to their undefeated season? He gained a nickname that day which stayed with him the rest of his life. And if any of you have ever heard of him, it is by the name, Wrong Way Riegal. That's the only thing he is ever remembered for or called. Even when he was an old man, and to his dying day he was called Wrong Way Riegal. It seems a little unfair doesn't it?

Now let me tell you about another man with a nickname who is also remembered for the one great stumbling mistake of his otherwise sterling and admirable life. His name was Thomas, one of Jesus' disciples and forever known down through history as "Doubting Thomas." In fact his name has become synonymous with doubt itself. This too is unfair, but worse it is slander on a devoted, good Christian man who helped to turn the world upside down for Jesus Christ, carried the Gospel to India, and was one of the few individuals to whom Jesus made a personal appearance after His resurrection during those fateful and wonderful forty days.

I. THOMAS THE CHOSEN DISCIPLE

We know nothing of the early life of Thomas, but we do know that the Lord Jesus chose and called him to be one of his inner circle of disciples, whom He would train to become the leaders of the early church. In fact the Lord spent all night in prayer before the choices were made. Later, when Jesus said to them, "Have not I chosen you twelve, but one of you is a devil?" He was not referring to faithful Thomas. He included Thomas in His great high priestly prayer in the garden, when He called the disciples, "Those who You, Father, have given Me out of the world. They were always Yours and You gave them to Me." Jesus never called him, "doubting Thomas."

Towards the very end, when the Lord announced to His disciples that He was going back to Jerusalem, they all protested that since the Jews were out to kill Him, He should not return there. However, Thomas simply said in all sincerity, "I'm going too that I may die with Him." Brave Thomas, faithful Thomas, maybe even gloomy Thomas, but call him not "Doubting Thomas," at least not at that moment, for he showed more courage and steadfastness than all the others put together. But when the showdown came, Thomas began to falter, and deep questions began to torment his brave mind.

II. THOMAS IN DOUBT

It began in the upper room during the last supper when Jesus began to say, "Let not your hearts be troubled...I am going to prepare a place for you, that where I am, there you may be also... and where I go you go, and the way you know." That was just too much for Thomas. His heart was broken when Jesus said He was going away. He did not know where the Lord was going and so he knew he could never find Him again. Even Jesus' words of reassurance failed to ease his mind or his troubled heart.

It got worse. When Jesus was arrested, and would not allow the disciples to defend Him, they all fled; even Thomas who had come to Jerusalem to die with Him. From afar Thomas saw His body hanging on the Roman cross, felt the earthquake, and experienced the awful darkness which fell at noon and lasted three long hours. But the un-natural darkness of the day was nothing compared to the darkness of his soul. Jesus had died. He was not the promised Messiah after all. He was not the Son of God. He was dead! The Father had not intervened and saved

Him. Dark billows of sorrow and unbelief overwhelmed the soul of Thomas.

And some of us have been right there with him. Confessors of Christ, church members, choir members, Sunday school teachers, elders, deacons, pastors...then stark and inexplicable tragedies have come out of nowhere, leaving us devastated and doubting. Look again at Thomas, and the added up reasons for his doubts and fears.

1. Confusion about what Jesus said there in the upper room. He simply could not put things together. In his mind, Jesus kept contradicting Himself, talking about a glorious kingdom and eternal life, then admitting He would soon die.

2. Personal failure. Brave, bold Thomas, who like Peter said he was willing to die for Jesus, finally ran like a rabbit when they took Jesus away in that dark garden. Oh how devastating for a believer to be shown his own sin and weakness, especially when we do the very things we have bragged about saying, "Well! I would never do that!" Then we do, and God seems far away and unreal.

3. Deep, crushing, personal sorrow; the death of a loved one; the death of Jesus. Thomas who had joyfully sung, "I have decided to follow Jesus" and "I'll go with Him, with Him all the way" would never again find it easy to believe.

III. THOMAS THE BELIEVER

When word began to filter out to the disciples that the tomb of Jesus was empty and that some of the women had seen Jesus alive, Thomas didn't fall for that hysteria, not even for a minute. "Why can't they accept the fact He is dead" thought Thomas. "Utter nonsense" said Thomas to those who told him what the women said. Then to make matters even worse, even John and Peter both told him they had seen and talked with the Lord. "What's got into them?" he thought. Then all ten of the former disciples came to Thomas and told him, Jesus had come to them and talked with them. With hot tears of bitter anger burning his eyes, Thomas retorted, "Unless I see in his hands the print of the nails, and put my finger into the print of the nails, and put my hand into the wound on His side, I will not believe!"

Now you may call him, "doubting Thomas." He had rejected the testimony of faithful witnesses. He had forgotten the things Jesus had said about dying and being raised from the dead. He refused to come together with other believers to worship and wait on the Lord. So he laid down his own conditions for God to meet if he was to ever again believe that Jesus was the Son of God, the Savior, and Thomas was sure those conditions would never be met.

Then Jesus came, and called Thomas by his very own name and said, "Look at Me, Thomas. Look and examine My wounds, touch My nail scarred hands, My spear-riven side. Do not be unbelieving, but believing." It's your choice now Thomas. Which will it be? A life of cynicism, doubt, rebellion and sin? Or a life of faith and faithfulness to Me?

Without hesitation, Thomas, who now had seen and handled the risen Lord, confessed with his mouth what he believed in his heart, that God the Father had raised God the Son, Jesus his Master and Lord from the dead. Thomas's words echo and resound throughout Christendom to this very day, and speak for you; what you want to say right now: "MY LORD AND MY GOD."

Now Jesus looks beyond Thomas and sees you sitting here right now. So He speaks once more through His word and Spirit, just to you. "Thomas, because you have seen Me you have believed, but blessed are those who have not seen and yet have believed." Will you accept the challenge? Will you inherit the blessing above all blessings? Say it now, say it from your heart, "MY LORD AND MY GOD."

For Discussion and Reflection

1. After reading this chapter, has your view of Thomas changed? Do you find that you can relate to him, or perhaps feel compassion for him? How so?

2. Why do you think Thomas doubted the other disciples?

3. What causes you to doubt? How do you wrestle with those things? How do you work your way from doubt to faith?

4. Can you proclaim, "My Lord and my God"? Why or why not?

10

The Missionary Mandate

~

MATTHEW 28

During the forty days between Jesus' resurrection and ascension into heaven, He met with His disciples on many occasions to remind them of all He had taught during His earthly ministry. It was during this time also He made very explicit one great truth for which He had been preparing them in several different ways over the three previous years. That one great truth was that His Gospel must be preached to all the nations of the world, and that the Kingdom would not be limited to the remnant of Jewish people who lived in Judea, or even among the dispersion scattered throughout the Roman Empire. It is true that in one of His last sermons before His death, the Lord Jesus did say that the Gospel of the Kingdom would be preached to all the nations of the world before His return, but now in this forty days period what had been a prophecy becomes an explicit mandate.

In all four of the Gospels and in the book of Acts, we discover that this missionary mandate occupies the most prominent place in the Gospel of the forty days. Luke tells about the Lord appearing to His disciples in the upper room the evening of the resurrection and opening their minds to understand the Scriptures concerning Himself. The Lord Jesus showed them from the Old Testament that it was necessary for the Messiah to suffer, die, and be raised again, and that this Gospel should be preached to all the nations. Somehow in all my years of study of this passage, it had escaped my notice that Jesus proved from the Old Testament that the Gospel must be proclaimed to the world. But listen again to these words: "Thus it is written, and thus it was necessary for the Christ to suffer and to rise from the dead the third day; and that repentance and remission of sins should be preached in His name to all the nations…"

In John's account, the risen Lord Jesus came to His disciples, stood in their midst and showed them His hands and His side. His spoken words were these: 1. "Peace be unto you," and 2. "As the Father has sent Me, I also send you." Please notice, this was one of the first things Jesus said to His disciples after greeting them and showing them He was indeed alive again. It is as if to say, "Since I am risen from the dead, go to the world with this message."

Now we come to the Great Commission as given in Matthew 28. Is there a contradiction here? Matthew reports this as occurring just before the Lord ascended into heaven, while Luke and John both tell us that Jesus said essentially the same thing on the very day of His resurrection. Of course there is no contradiction! Rather a repetition for emphasis. It was the first thing He said to His disciples after His resurrection, AND the last thing He told them before His ascension. So we begin to get the idea this was at the very top of Christ's priorities, and it must be so for His Church. Unfortunately, it is often the last.

I. THE SETTING & THE FOUNDATION FOR THE GREAT COMMISSION

As the time drew near for Jesus to return to His Father and to the throne of Heaven, He gathered His disciples to a mountain in Galilee, and gave His final command. Notice the tender kindness of Jesus in bringing His disciples to a mountain for this event. It was on a mountain He had first ordained them as apostles. It was on a mountain He preached His greatest sermon. It was on a mountain He allowed Peter, James, and John to behold His glory as He conversed with Moses and Elijah about His approaching death. What wonderful memories this must have brought to their minds and hearts to meet Him once more on a lovely mountain.

We are told that when they saw Him, they worshiped Him, but some doubted. O how stubborn is unbelief. One thing of which I am completely sure. At this encounter, Thomas could not be numbered among the doubters. We have already heard him exclaim to the risen Savior, "My Lord and my God." Perhaps it had been several days since His last appearance. Maybe some were thinking, "It's just too good to be true."

It is also obvious that when Jesus spoke, they put whatever doubts they had behind them. His first words were, "All power in heaven and earth is given unto Me." He had previously made this claim, before His death on the cross, but events seemed to have made it an impossible dream. In the intervening time He was rejected, tried, condemned and crucified, dead, and buried. Now however, who could deny His authority or His claim to equality with the Father. He was alive again! Many prophets and great men had gone before Him in death, including Abraham, Moses, David, Elijah and Elisha, Isaiah, Jeremiah, and Daniel. But none had risen from the dead. Here He is alive and gloriously transformed. Never again would He be the lowly Jesus of humiliation, but the exalted Christ, the Lord from heaven. Jesus is claiming all power and authority. During His earthly ministry He exercised great power by his miracles of healing, casting out demons, even raising the dead to life again. But He always exercised restraint as well as power. He would not call upon the twelve legions of angels to save Him from death. At times He told those whom He had healed to tell no man.

From this moment on His power would be unrestricted save by His own will. This authority will include the raising of all the dead, either to glory or to everlasting shame and punishment. He will also sit upon His throne of judgment and call all men and nations before Him to give an account of their lives. His word will be final. All whom He rejects will be banished forever from His presence and His heaven. All whom He accepts will inherit the kingdom and a closeness with Him from which they will never be separated. It is upon this claim of all power and authority He issues His great command to the waiting apostles and to all who claim Him as Lord.

II. THE GREAT COMMISSION EXAMINED

Let us examine this command with great care and with full intention to obey it with all our hearts. Here is what Jesus said: "Go therefore and make disciples of all nations, baptizing them in the name of the Father and of the Son and of the Holy Spirit, teaching them to observe all things that I have commanded you…"

The words "go into all the world" are both broad and deep. The church is not to overemphasize either "come" or "go" but to fully emphasize both! Of course you must come to Christ and abide with Him and in Him before you may go to the world, but most are content to come to Christ, and only a few seem eager to go. We probably are very good at saying to people, "come to church," but very weak in "going out to seek the lost." The church is so often confused about its mission in the world. But our confusion is not derived from the teachings of our Lord and His disciples, but from our reluctance to obey, and our compromise with the world. "Go into all the world" is the command in light of the earlier words of Jesus, "This gospel of the kingdom will be preached in all the world." I believe that the command, "go into all the world" means more than just geography. I believe we are to penetrate all levels of human culture and society with the saving gospel and the teachings of our Lord, as well as reaching out to all nations and peoples.

The command, "teaching them to observe all things that I have commanded you" includes preaching the gospel to all people everywhere, as the disciples surely did. It also means teaching them to observe all things our Lord taught so that we may say with the apostle Paul, "Therefore I testify to you that I am innocent of the blood of all men, for I have not failed to declare to you the whole counsel of God." Just preaching the Gospel without also "making disciples" is really not preaching the Gospel. Perhaps this accounts for the evaluation of the church in America that it is a mile wide and an inch deep.

An eager young college student returned from a week's mission trip bubbling over with great joy. He told us that as he walked down the street in a large Asian city and handed out tracts, people were accepting Christ left and right. He was somewhat sobered by a conversation he had with a very polite young Asian, when he asked him to "Pray after me these words," and he eagerly did so. Then when the prayer was over this new convert told my college friend: "Thank you, now I am a Christian, a Hindu and Buddhist, and a Moslem, surely I will go to heaven."

Our Lord Jesus did not spend three years of intensive teaching His disciples just for their enlightenment and enjoyment, but also to equip them to fulfill the Great Commission by teaching all these things to the nations of the world. How are we doing?

That the Great Commission includes avid and prayerful evangelism is obvious when He included, "Baptizing them in the name of the Father, and of the Son, and of the Holy Spirit." This implies an understanding of the nature of the great Triune God, and His purpose and will as Creator, Sustainer, and Redeemer; all of which is included in biblical evangelism. Of course evangelism includes, "Christ died for our sins," which means it is our duty to teach and preach the necessity of repentance from sin. But it also includes, "In the beginning, God created the heavens and the earth," and all that implies.

III. THE INCREDIBLE PROMISE

What an undertaking! This command was given to a small handful of people long ago, but who will deny it is intended as the marching orders, the mandate for the whole Church until our Lord comes again. How is it possible when it seems so utterly impossible now as much as then? There is but one answer, and this is found in the incredible promise Christ gave to encourage and enable us in our assigned task. "Lo, I am with you always, even to the end of the age."

Let me rephrase this in an attempt to capture the fullness and wonder of this promise. "Consider this: I Myself will be with you always, day after day, moment by moment, and My grace will be sufficient, for I will never leave you nor forsake you, and great will be your reward in heaven, even if you lay down your life for the Gospel's sake."

So that's the mandate, and that's the promise of our Lord, the great Head of the church. If we are to justify our existence, if we are to expect God's continued blessing on all our efforts, we must be faithful, true, and obedient to His great commission.

For Discussion and Reflection

1. In this chapter, we read that the mandate to "go into all the world" is "more than just geography." What are some ways in which we can "go into all the world" without crossing beyond the borders of our individual communities?

2. What authority did Jesus pass on to us in the Great Commission? How are you applying that authority in your efforts to "go into all the world"?

3. The Great Commission includes the command to baptize. Why is baptism essential to discipleship?

4. Study the other accounts of this commission (Mark 16:14-20, Luke 24:36-49, John 20:19-22, Acts 1:4-8). What do all have in common? What differences do you find? What did Jesus teach that we must do to in order to be His disciples?

11

Words of Love and Great Power

MATTHEW 28:18-20

It had been forty days since Jesus was raised from the dead, but now the time had come for Him to return to the Father and begin His high priestly ministry in preparation for His return to claim the crown and to be recognized as "King of kings and Lord of lords forever and ever."

These were days of glory and it was absolutely necessary to convince the disciples that He had risen indeed and that as such He was proven to be what He had claimed to be, God the Son equal with God the Father; as He said, "I and My Father are one." And it was just as important to also prove that He was and is and ever shall be "The Son of Man." Thus God and man now joined together in one person and two natures forever. "Seeing then that we have a great high priest, that is passed into the heavens, Jesus the Son of God, let us hold fast our profession. For we have not a high priest who cannot be touched with the feelings of our infirmities: but was tempted in all points like as we are, yet without sin. Let us therefore come boldly unto the throne of grace, that we may obtain mercy and find grace to help in times of need."

It was just as important for the disciples then and now to understand that once God also became man He remains both God and man forever. During those fabulous forty days He taught them many things. We all have rejoiced in His resurrection from the dead which we celebrate at Easter, but every Lord's Day we come together to acknowledge His resurrection and His abiding presence by the Holy Spirit. And well we should, but we have also considered all He taught His disciples by word and deed during these glory days. And this, beloved, in many ways has been the most overlooked of all that Jesus said and did, and at the same time one of the most important parts of the whole Bible; and we are spiritually impoverished by overlooking and neglecting His teaching during these forty days. He affirmed that the whole Old Testament, the law, the prophets, and the psalms were all about Him, and that He was and is the perfect fulfillment of all the Scriptures. He taught them many other things too numerous to mention here and now, but as we learned, He gave to the Church her highest and most urgent task, the Missionary Mandate--His highest priority for her, yet far, far down the list for many if not most Christians. He told us that the highest purpose of the church was to preach the Gospel and make disciples of all the nations. (He also promised that when the Gospel had been preached around the world, He would return in power and great glory.)

Now we come to almost the last thing he taught His church then and now before He was taken up to heaven in His glorious ASCENSION. Listen carefully to these words: "BAPTIZING THEM IN THE NAME OF THE FATHER AND OF THE SON AND OF THE HOLY GHOST." The Lord left us with two sacraments, Baptism and the Lord's Supper, to bind us together as His family. As a testimony to our fallen nature and to our perverse thinking, we have allowed His two marks of our unity with Him and each other to become the most divisive expression of our disunity with Him and each other. And the reasons for this are not hard to discover: 1. Our ungodly pride, and 2. our focus on the elements rather than the words. In our pride and ignorance we turn the Lord's intention to express our unity with Him and each other into symbols of arrogant disdain by proving we are right and everyone else is wrong. We would rather argue about the amount of water it takes to symbolize the cleansing the Holy Spirit brings than to experience the cleansing and accept the grace.

We also take pleasure in arguing about who should be baptized and when, and we are adept at finding scriptures which seem to support our position, whatever that might be, rather than obeying His command that we love one another. In both the sacraments of Baptism and the Lord's Supper the elements have their place, but to ascribe salvation to the elements is to totally misunderstand the meaning of these two precious reminders of our Savior and our salvation. For instance to ascribe salvation to baptism per se is ruinous to our walk with the Lord, just as in the Lord's Supper it borders on idolatry to think that by eating and drinking the elements we are truly receiving Christ into our hearts and lives.

Today the real question is: What did the risen Lord mean when He said in Matt 28:19, "Go therefore and teach all nations, baptizing them in the name of the Father, and of the Son and of the Holy Ghost; teaching them to observe all that I have commanded you?" The main verb is "make disciples;" the method is "baptizing them" and "teaching them." This is how to make disciples and this adds depth to these two lesser verbs. That baptism involves true repentance and true faith in the Savior is obvious. When the Philippian jailor asked, "What must I do to be saved?" Paul answered, "Believe in the Lord Jesus Christ, and you will be saved." Then Paul spent the rest of the night explaining repentance and the meaning of faith in the Lord Jesus Christ; after which the man and all his household were baptized. To be ready for baptism requires repentance and hearing the word of the Gospel and receiving the Lord Jesus as Savior and Lord; anything less would make baptism a sort of magical rite rather than a sign of repentance and faith.

Baptism implies a break with the world and the beginning of a new life centered in that special relationship with God as revealed in His word. What does it mean to say "baptizing them in the name of the Father and of the Son and of the Holy Ghost"? Note well the Lord Jesus did not say in the "names" plural but into the "name" singular, for there is one God revealed in the Trinity. But what does it mean to say "in the name"? Go with me to the Gospel of John and hear what Jesus said when He prayed for His disciples and for us. He said to the Father, "Keep them in Thy name," and again, "While I was with them I kept them in Thy name..." What does this mean and how does it relate to baptizing them in the name of the Father and of the Son and of the Holy Ghost? The name of God is all the truth about His nature and His work of salvation in our behalf. The Lord Jesus was claming that He had taught His disciples the whole truth of God, all that His glorious name implies. So when we baptize people in God's holy name, we baptize them into all the truth of God as revealed in His word, and especially the truth about our Lord Jesus.

We also bind them to be his faithful disciples willing to live and die for Him. Doesn't this elevate the truth of baptism to a much higher level than the endless disputes concerning water: how much, who, and when? I am not saying that the act of baptism is unimportant. What I am saying is it is more important to understand and meditate on the WORDS of baptism than the questions of WATER.

The next truths of the Gospel of forty days are the actual ascension of Jesus Christ to the right hand of God the Father and the thrill of knowing "From thence He shall come again to judge the quick and the dead."

For Discussion and Reflection

1. "For we have not a high priest who cannot be touched with the feelings of our infirmities, but was tempted in all points like as we are, yet without sin." Meditate on this truth that Jesus felt pain and suffered as we do; He knew what it was to walk in our shoes. Reflect upon what this means in terms of the depth of His mercy, compassion, and love. How does it affect your idea of the concept of Jesus walking beside you?

2. Review this chapter with these two questions in mind: (1) What was it about Jesus' teaching during the Great Forty Days that was so critically important to His mission? (2) What did he tell His disciples was the highest purpose of the Church?

3. What is necessary in order for a person to be truly ready for baptism? What is the significance of baptizing in the name of the Trinity?

4. In order to make disciples, we must first be disciples. What does it mean to be a disciple of Jesus?

12

This Same Jesus Shall Return

∼

ACTS 1:1-11
LUKE 21:25-28

When the Lord Jesus had completed His earthly ministry He led his disciples out to the Mount of Olives. After a few brief words including a repetition of the Great Commission, while His disciples watched, He was lifted up and began to ascend from earth to heaven. They were too overwhelmed to do anything but continue to gaze steadfastly into heaven until a low flying cloud received Him out of their sight. Still they looked and still they wondered at this amazing sight. Were they hoping against hope that the cloud would pass or part and that once more they would see Jesus?

Suddenly two men stood with them, dressed in white brilliance, obviously heavenly beings, angels in fact. They broke the silence by asking, "You men of Galilee, why do you stand gazing up into heaven? This same Jesus who was taken from you into heaven will so come in like manner as you saw go into heaven." That was all that was said, then the angels disappeared and the disciples were left alone. They went back to Jerusalem and found a quiet safe quiet place and then reflected on what had happened those last precious forty days. They tried to remember all that He had said just before He was taken up and away. He told them to wait in Jerusalem for a few days until the Father fulfilled His promise that Jesus had so emphatically told them when He said; "Wait in Jerusalem until the promise of the Father is fulfilled and you shall receive power after the Holy Spirit is poured out upon you."

Then they began to reflect on what the angels had told them, and especially these words: "This same Jesus who was taken up from you into heaven will so come in like manner as you have seen Him go into heaven." As they thought upon these words their wonder and joy greatly increased. "This same Jesus will come again." Wonderful words of life!

"THIS SAME JESUS" whose birth, life, death and resurrection was foreseen by the law, prophets and Psalms.

Who was conceived in the womb of the Virgin Mary and born of her yet without sin.

Who was born in a stable in Bethlehem and whose first bed was a manger where the sheep and cattle were fed.

Who was a Child of the Covenant and whose body bore the marks of that Covenant.

Who at the age of twelve, and due to his presence in the temple courts (Luke 2:46), most likely formally accepted the responsibility of keeping that Covenant by showing Himself to be a "Son of the Law" or under the law. And for the first time Someone took those vows and actually obeyed the law in letter and spirit.

Who was set aside to His public ministry by the prophet John the Baptist who declared Him to be the Messiah and the Lamb of God who takes away the sin of the world.

Who was driven by the Spirit into the wilderness to fast and pray and was there tempted and tried by the evil one in all points as we are, yet was without sin and is therefore our great High Priest who understands the feelings of our infirmities, so that we may come to the throne of grace that we may obtain mercy and find grace to help in our times of need.

Who healed the sick even of leprosy, cast out evil spirits, stilled the troubled waters of Galilee by calming the storm tossed sea and yes, raised the dead, and claimed that He would raise all the dead one day either to spend eternity with Him in God's heaven, or be eternally committed to the flames of hell.

Who gathered around Him twelve men to train for the task of preaching His gospel to the ends of the earth and time; though they would all forsake Him: betrayed by one and also denied by another, His best friend.

Who spent His last night on earth observing the Passover and gloriously transforming it into the new Passover, the Lord's Supper.

Who went to the Garden of Gethsemane to beseech the Father to spare Him the dreadful cup of God's wrath. He begged God three times during this ordeal saying, "O My Father if it be possible, let this cup pass from Me," but each time surrendered to the Father's will and ended by saying, "If this cup may not pass away from Me except I drink it, Thy will be done."

Who was arrested and was taken to trial before the Jewish Sanhedrin and, though adored by the common folk, was despised by the leaders of God's people who insisted that the Roman governor Pontius Pilate crucify Him; and though he declared Jesus to be not guilty and that He had done nothing worthy to be condemned, still gave in and sent Him to the cross and death.

Who was beaten and brutalized, mocked, and scorned by the Jews and the Romans and was nailed to the cross while praying, "Father forgive them for they know not what they do." When one of the criminals who was executed with Him sought forgiveness from Jesus, he was assured by the Savior, "Today you will be with Me in paradise."

Who when He saw His mother suffering for His sake committed her to the care of faithful John who accepted Jesus' charge to Him.

Who after three suffering hours on the cross endured another dreadful three hours when He who knew no sin became sin for us that we might become the righteousness of God in Him. A great darkness fell on the earth, but a greater darkness fell on His soul forcing him to cry with pain and agony, "My God, why have you forsaken Me?"

Who when the debt for our sins was fully paid, said, "It is finished, Father into your hands I commend my Spirit."

Then He died and was buried in the tomb of Joseph of Arimathaea. There He was to remain until in the early dawn of Sunday morning the Father raised Him from the dead, having accepted His sacrifice.

Who spent forty remarkable days showing Himself alive to His disciples by many infallible proofs. Then just before He ascended into heaven the Lord Jesus assigned to the disciples then and now the task of preaching the Gospel and making disciples.

They saw Him ascend into heaven. He was gone. They stared into space no doubt hoping He would return. But then two angels came to these bewildered and heartbroken men with a message that echoes today in our ears and gives hope and confidence and a reason to live: "You men of Galilee why are you gazing into heaven? This same Jesus whom you saw ascend into heaven will so come again in like manner as you have seen Him ascend into heaven."

Did you hear what they said? Do you believe it? Are you ready for Him to come or are you still clinging to your sinful ways while feebly saying, "But I believe in Jesus!" If you do then bring forth the fruits of repentance and true faith before it is too late. This same Jesus forgave and transformed Peter into what Jesus knew he would become. And he can do the same with you. But you have to ask Him and be truly willing to repent and become what the Lord Jesus wants you to.

Who when the debt was fully paid said, "It is finished, into Thy hands I commend my spirit."

For Discussion and Reflection

1. How does a right understanding of the glory of Christ and His approaching return create a sense of urgency to obey the Great Commission and "make disciples of all nations"? How can you cultivate this determination in your own life, in your family, and in your congregation?

2. How do you think Jesus' disciples were affected by the promise that he would return? How are you affected by that promise?

3. How do prayer and study help you anticipate the coming of Christ?

4. How is God using you to be a witness to His life, death, resurrection, and continuing ministry?

13

The Judge of All the Earth

MATTHEW 25:31-46

Note: Although the Lord did not directly include the doctrine of the last judgment in the forty day period between His resurrection and His ascension, yet this account of the final judgment belongs as a part of His post resurrection ministry because it is strongly implied in all He said and did during this time.

Jesus told four stories to explain and reinforce the great importance of believing that He is coming again, and of being prepared and ready for that day and hour when He returns. The first three stories are in the form of parables, simple little stories of what happened to people, some who were prepared and some unprepared, for one grand event and accounting for responsibilities and opportunities given them. He spoke of the joy and full blessings for those prepared, and the bitter loss for the unprepared.

The last story He told was not a parable, but a vivid description of what it will be like when all people and nations stand before His judgment seat on that last day. When you first begin to read this last story, you think you are reading another parable, but then suddenly you realize two things. 1. It is not a parable but a description of an actual event. 2. You are right in the middle of that story yourself. One way or another it's about you and what will happen when you appear before the judgment seat of Christ. That totally changes how you read, hear, and think about this last story.

Do you realize there will one day and hour be an end to all things as we have known them? Do you understand that there will come a day when all that Christ described in His great sermon on the end of the world will actually happen? Do you see how all the movements of history are even now leading up to that grand and terrible event? Listen again to the dramatic, yet simple announcement: "When the Son of Man comes in His glory, and all the angels with Him, then He shall sit on His throne of glory." Justice demands it. Reason requires it. The Word of God assures it. Conscience confirms it. Deep down in your heart you know you will have to answer to God for the way you have lived your life.

I. THE ONE WHO WILL JUDGE

Jesus Christ, God the Son, is the One who will sit on the glorious judgment throne. This must be the case. Once He appeared before the judgment seats of mankind. He was arrested in the Garden of Gethsemane. He was brutally treated in an illegal trial by night before the high priest, and the elders of the people who made up the highest court of the Jews. He was slapped, spit upon, blindfolded, falsely accused, ridiculed, and at last judged to be such a vile sinner as to deserve death. He was taken before the Roman judge Pontius Pilate who found Him not guilty, but for fear of losing his influence and position sentenced Him to be cruelly crucified. He was mocked and tortured by the Roman soldiers, who whipped him, crammed a vicious crown of thorns on His head, and then nailed Him to a cross to suffer and die. The world rejected Him, judged Him to be a wicked sinner, and put Him to death.

But God raised Him from the dead, and gave Him the name which is above all names, and appointed Him to be the judge of all men and angels at the last day. Even now at the Father's right hand He rules and also intercedes for His own for whom He died. But when He comes again, all people of all nations and ages will confess that He is both Lord and Judge. They will see Him in all His magnificent power and glory, and in His unflinching justice and terrible wrath against sin and sinners.

God is a holy and righteous God. No sin will ever go unpunished, and if your sin was not punished in the body of Jesus on Calvary's cross, it will be punished beginning on that last day and then forever. Christ must sit on the judgment throne to vindicate God's righteousness, and His own. The world's last word about Jesus was that He was a guilty sinner deserving of death, and that was and is a base lie which must be exposed as such. All humanity must see Him for whom and what He really is. The sentence of the world must be overturned by a higher court. And it will be.

II. THERE MUST BE SEPARATION BETWEEN THE SAVED AND THE LOST

The Bible makes a very strong point from Genesis through Revelation that there must be a difference between God's people and the people of the world; between the seed of the woman and the seed of the serpent. "Come out from among them and be separate, saith your God" is the constant call of God's word, Old and New Testaments. The word warns us against being too much a part of this world and its values and ideals. When we see Christ on the throne of judgment, we will know why this is so important.

The wheat and tares may grow together in the same field and at first bear a striking resemblance to each other. But at the time of harvest the difference will appear, and they will be separated by the reapers. We somehow like to think this ultimate separation will never take place, and that there will always be a vague and hazy line between good and evil, right and wrong. People love to talk about "shades of grey," but with God it is always black and white, right and wrong, good and evil. God's people seem to always resist the call of Scripture to be a holy people, and to live by different standards from the world.

Jesus said, "Before Him shall be gathered all the nations of the world, and He shall separate them from each other, as the shepherd separates the sheep from the goats." You may not like that, but you will like it even less when it happens. This means all people, and each individual will come before Christ's glorious judgment throne. At His command, there will be a clear and final separation between those who are His and those who are not. One of the most sad things about this is that in another sermon of Jesus, the one we call the Sermon on the Mount, Jesus said that many who claim to be His are not, and will discover this to their everlasting regret and sorrow.

The basis for the separation is clear. Those whose earthly lives give clear evidence of faith in the Lord Jesus Christ, who live in harmony with His will, as seen in their obedience to His commands and His example; these and these alone will be gathered to Him as a shepherd gathers his sheep. In particular their righteousness is seen in their deeds of mercy towards those in need. "I was hungry and you fed me; thirsty and you gave me drink; I was a stranger, and you took me in; I was naked and you clothed me; I was sick and you visited me; I was in prison and you came to Me."

O listen to me parents of children. Your little ones are hungry for the word, thirsty for the truth of salvation, naked apart from the righteousness of Christ to cover their sins, faced with a dark prison of ignorance of God's word. Have you fed them upon the bread of life, given them to drink of the fountain of grace, clothed them and guarded them with a knowledge of the Savior? Shown them an example of how believers deal with problems and disappointments in life?

Those who have lived in rebellion against Him and have ignored His love and His laws, either by outright rejection, insincere profession, or futile attempts at neutrality, will be identified as "goats" and placed on His left hand as a sign of supreme and final rejection and designation for punishment. But primarily the test comes again at the point of how you respond to those in dire need. Is your heart one with the Savior, or in captivity to the spirit of this world?

III. THERE WILL BE A TIME OF REVELATION AND JUDGMENT

Another obvious point Christ was making is that there will be a time of revelation and justice. By this I mean, evil will be seen for what it is. All sham and pretense will be stripped away. Good will no longer be reviled and ridiculed. All hidden and unknown evil will be revealed, and all goodness will be brought to light. All undiscovered and unsolved crimes will be made known, and all deeds hidden by the darkness of night will be exposed to the light of day. Every vile and hateful word and thought will be, in the words of Christ, "shouted from the housetops." Every failure will be made known. Cold indifference or persecution of God's people will be dealt with. Indeed this is the one example of punishable sins Christ uses in this sermon. All lies will be exposed for what they are, even the ones we convince ourselves are true. Every minister of the Gospel must account for the things he has spoken in the name of Christ, and every church member will answer for each word heard. We must answer for the vows we have taken and either kept or disobeyed.

True believers in Christ will be identified, justified, accepted in the presence of all men and angels. They will be extolled by the true Judge and praised for their faithfulness and good works. They will be called "Blessed of the Father" and welcomed into eternal joy and reward.

Just think what it would be like for the Lord, King Jesus to call your name before all the assembled throngs of heaven and earth to hear, and welcome you home.

And they will be absolutely astonished! For they are those who are humbled by their own sin and failure, and for the most part unaware that their loving concern for others is that important. They have just lived in lowly and even unconscious awareness that they have been ministering to the Lord Jesus, as they have ministered to the needy and outcasts and have gone about their seemingly insignificant lives day by day living out the love and mercy of the Lord Jesus without fanfare or self-adulation.

All others will be rebuked, accused, and condemned. They will be called "cursed" by the only One who could have saved them. The very One they rejected and despised. At last there will be no question whose we are and whom we serve.

At this point the words of Psalm 130 ring in our ears, "If You Lord should mark iniquity, O Lord who could stand." We are forced to face ourselves, before we must face the One true Judge. Our only hope is in the shed blood of the Lamb, His forgiveness and His righteousness given to us. When true conversion takes place in a person's heart, Christ becomes both Savior and Lord. Is He truly reigning in your heart? Are you preparing for that day and hour when you will be called before Him by the often times slow but discernable process of sanctification…and it is a process, and often slow, but in spite of setbacks, it is sure.

IV. THERE WILL BE A FINAL PLACE OF DESTINY FOR ALL

This is the grand finale. This is the end towards which all are moving. These are the two paths upon which all are now walking…one or the other. Both are final, both irrevocable. It will either be "Come ye blessed of My Father, inherit the kingdom prepared for you from before the foundation of the earth" or "Depart from Me ye cursed, into everlasting fire prepared for the devil and his angels." But the choice must be made, and wisdom dictates that it should be made now. And choices and decisions we make every day in small things, as well as life ordering or life altering decisions, should include the eternal dimensions as suggested by this sermon of Christ.

THE SERIOUSNESS OF LIFE

As we conclude our consideration of this sermon of Christ, His conclusion in a way rules out what we think is the vast importance of millennial distinctives. What really is important is the influence this sermon should have on the way we live right here and now, both as individuals and as a congregation of God's people. One thing which hits me with such great force is the need for ministry of outreach and service to the "least of Christ's brothers and sisters." Often much of the church's attention is focused internally, and that's not all bad, and is in fact very necessary. But the time is upon us when we need to think of our identification in terms of what use we are in the kingdom. If we are truly to be Christ's Church, let's keep in mind this final sermon as we plan our ministry and seek to serve in His name and for His sake. Of course our first priority must always center in true worship and faithfully proclaiming the word of God, but saying this does not in any way lessen the importance of giving due and urgent consideration to the implications of this text to the community around us and to the many crying needs of hurting people. Even as Christ put windows of illuminating illustrations in His sermons, so we must put windows of loving concern for people in the ministry Christ has assigned to us. .

For Discussion and Reflection

1. What do you think of the behaviors listed in this chapter that will mark some as "goats"? Do any of these surprise you? What about the idea that "God's people seem to always resist the call of Scripture to be a holy people"? How do you experience this resistance in your personal life, in your congregation, and among your friends and business associates?

2. How did you feel when you read that God does not see in shades of gray, but rather in black and white? Does the idea cause you to be fearful? Why?

3. "Is He truly reigning in your heart?" Ponder this question with brutal honesty. Pray about it. Journal about it. Study Psalm 130, then make it your daily prayer.

4. "Choices and decisions we make every day in small things ... should include the eternal dimensions as suggested by this sermon of Christ." How can you adopt this into your consciousness and make it a guide for everyday living? How can it inform your ministry in the world as a disciple of Christ?

Postscript

Factual truth is the foundation for faith. Christianity is founded upon actual events which occurred in history and were recorded by reliable and faithful witnesses. From a historian's perspective you can be just as sure that Jesus Christ rose again from the dead after His crucifixion as you can be that Julius Caesar crossed the Rubicon and made his way to Rome to take over the reins of government and become the first real Emperor. The Resurrection of Jesus Christ on the third day can be just as firmly established as an historical event as the fall of Constantinople, and the end of the Eastern Roman Empire. The empty tomb is certainly as well documented as the defeat of Napoleon at Waterloo, or Lee at Gettysburg.

No matter how adamantly one may insist that the resurrection is "merely" an article of faith, the truth is that when the same historical criterion is applied as is used to establish the historicity of any other human event, the resurrection stands the test and objectively takes its place in the actual recorded history of the human race.

Let me mention just one often overlooked but powerful testimony to the resurrection from hostile and negative sources: the reaction of Christ's enemies to the news brought by the Roman guards placed at the tomb of Jesus to prevent His disciples from stealing the dead body of their Lord. The Gospels record the reaction of these guards to the earthquake, the appearance of super natural beings (angels) at the tomb, and their fainting dead away with fright. When they recovered, they found the tomb empty and went immediately to the chief priest with their startling report. They in turn gathered the Sanhedrin together and quickly concocted a plan to counteract what they feared would be a terrible blow to their apparently successful effort to do away with Jesus. They gave a large bribe to the guards to persuade them to make up a story that His disciples came by night and stole Him away while they slept. They also promised the guards they would make things right with Pilate if he heard the story. The fact they felt it necessary to pay such a large bribe to the guards to do their bidding is very strong evidence they believed the guards' account of what happened and were fearful of the consequences. Nowadays we call this damage control.

But in saying all this to you, I am simply "preaching to the choir" so to speak, because most of you reading this already believe in the resurrection. But are you convinced enough to boldly proclaim and defend it before a hostile and unbelieving world? If we do not boldly stand upon this truth we may as well join the chorus of unbelief. My purpose in this postscript is to help you understand the significance of this great event for your faith and life by reminding you how the resurrection affected certain people who were dealing with the same issues you face every day.

After His resurrection, our Lord appeared to many people, sometimes individually and sometimes in groups of up to 500 people at one time. But I want to focus first and foremost on just three individuals; one overwhelmed with grief, one overcome with deep doubts, and one overwhelmed by personal failure.

In all three of these cases, the Lord answered their needs by proving to them He was alive and risen from the dead, and that made all the difference needed in their lives.

I. HE APPEARED TO MARY WEEPING INCONSOLABLY WITH GRIEF

There is no more poignant, heart-clutching scene in all the Bible than this: Mary weeping by the garden tomb of Jesus because she was unable to find His dead body and do the last thing she would ever be able to do to honor Him--the preparation of His body for final interment. There is just something about a woman weeping that reaches the depth of our emotions. As a pastor I have witnessed many tears from many women for many reasons. The man goes off to war to serve his country, and falls on the field of battle. His pain and fears are ended, but those of his wife or his mother have just begun. She will weep the rest of her life for many reasons, not the least of which, she could not be there to console and comfort him in his dying moments. I have witnessed the tears of many women whose husbands died before them, or the more bitter tears of those abandoned by their husbands, or broken-hearted over erring children. But the grief of Mary that Easter morning seemed to capture the heartache and tears of all women for all time. Defeat, anguish, and despair had crushed her. Not only was her Lord and healer dead, but even His poor mangled body had been stolen away. For her there could be no closure, and no end to her tears.

No doubt the kindly gardener meant well when he came up behind her and gently asked, "Woman, why are you weeping? Whom are you seeking?" Maybe it was the gentle tone of his voice which prompted her to respond, "Sir if you have carried Him away, tell me where you have laid Him, and I will take Him away." Surely if anyone knew where His body was, it would be the caretaker. There was a pause as she turned partly around and strained to see this man through the mist of the early morning.

He stepped closer and said simply, "Mary." The Good Shepherd called His sheep by name, and she heard His voice.

Then Mary, turning all the way around, knew Him, fell at His feet and worshiped Him, tried to cling to Him so He would never, never leave her again. But He said to her (gently again), "Cease clinging to Me, Mary, for I ascend to My Father and to your Father, to my God and to your God." Now she knew. He was the same Lord she had known before, but now gloriously alive forever. Death and the sorrow of death had lost its power to ruin her life. Now she had comfort for every sorrow she would still face. Now she had joy that would not be denied. Now she had hope that would not fail. For Christ is risen, He is risen indeed. And His words of assurance meant she too would rise one day and ascend to her Father, and to her God, and her Lord Jesus would be there also.

So if you are trapped in the pit of grief and despair, the Risen Savior is ready to reveal Himself to you through His word and by His Holy Spirit, and deliver you from that bondage of sorrow.

II. HE APPEARED TO THOMAS, DEFEATED BY DEEP DOUBTS

No doubt the grief of Thomas was real and as deep as Mary's. But his grief expressed itself not so much in inconsolable tears, but in the loss of faith and trust in the reality of what he had heard Jesus promise. When Thomas saw Jesus cruelly abused and executed in extreme pain and shame, all his faith and hope fled. His erstwhile confidence in all those beautiful and wonderful things Jesus had promised was lost. Never again, he thought, will I ever believe that He was going away to prepare a place for me. Never again could Thomas hope for a kingdom of righteousness and joy. How could he, after what they did to Jesus? Now he believed simply this: Jesus had been defeated. When a man is dead He is dead. Because he saw Him on a cross, with a crown of thorns on His head, he knew He would never

POSTSCRIPT

sit upon the throne of David and bring in the eternal kingdom. There was just too much evidence to the contrary, and he had seen it with his own eyes, and heard it with his own ears.

No matter how slender the cord, most people still hold on to the hope that Jesus was all He claimed to be, and that He was right about heaven and the conquest of death. But when bad things happen, and keep going on forever it seems, and when dark clouds of tragedy invade your life, and sorrows like sea billows roll, it becomes very difficult, and almost impossible, to hold on to faith and hope. And that doubt, that cynicism, would even make sense, except for one thing: "On the third day, He arose again from the dead." The event is so well established, and as I read I Corinthians 15, the meaning becomes more and more profound. Though I have never put my finger into the nail prints in His hands, nor thrust my hand into the spear wound in His side, I hear Him invite Thomas to do just this. But Thomas has now seen and heard, and no longer needs any other convincing. Then I hear Him say to me, "Blessed are those who have not seen, and yet believe." So I say to you, dear Lord Jesus, "Lord I believe, help Thou my unbelief. By your resurrection, doubts have lost their power to ruin my joy."

III. HE APPEARED TO PETER, CRUSHED BY THE REALIZATION OF HIS FAILURE

"But what does the risen Christ have for one who has failed so miserably, when I was so sure of His own sincerity and faith? What does the risen Savior offer a miserable sinner like me? I had boldly proclaimed my loyalty to Jesus Christ. I had promised myself over and over again that I would be true to Him, no matter what may come or how much it might cost. I had even decided that I love Him more than anyone else could possibly love Him. But then not once, nor twice, but in my case, three times, by word and deed done or left undone, I denied Him in the presence of His enemies and mine. I may as well forget it. He'll never want me back again. I may as well go back to the old life again.

"But then some hysterical women came running into the place of my misery, telling me He had risen from the dead and He sends word to His disciples, and especially to me, Peter, that He will meet them in Galilee.

"With John, we rushed to the tomb and found it empty, and the grave clothes laid aside. With wonder and even a slowly growing joy, we left the tomb and called together the others, except for Judas of course, and Thomas who didn't come, not at first. Suddenly He was there saying that simple but wonderful word He used so often before, 'Shalom.' But I still could not look him in the eyes. I knew He was risen and alive even as He promised, but I still could not believe He would ever want me back again. So the next day, I went back to my boat and my nets and took up where I had left off before He called me to become a fisher of men. How joyless and how empty was my heart…just like the nets I let down again and again all night, in vain. We started back but someone called us from the shore and told us to cast our nets on the other side. It was a hopeless gesture, but we did it anyway. Suddenly the nets were full, the boat almost sinking from the weight of fish, and John said, 'It is the Lord'; just like that first time three years or more before when we heard Him say, 'Follow me, and I will make you to become fishers of men.'

"I went to Him, miserable failure that I am, and He asked me a simple but, for me, heart-wrenching question. Using my old name before He gave me the new one, He said, 'Simon, son of John, do you love me more than these?' 'Yes Lord,' I said, with tears beginning to fill my eyes, 'You know that I love You. 'Feed my lambs,' was all He said. As the breakfast meal was ending, He asked the same question, and I gave Him the same answer. This time He replied, 'Shepherd My sheep.' One more time He asked His question. Doesn't He believe me? I wondered. How my heart was grieved. But from deep, deep down I was able to say, 'Lord, You know all things, You know I love You.' Once more it was simply: 'Feed My sheep.'

"Then it dawned on me, I am forgiven! I am set free from my guilt! I am restored, and He wants me to follow him and fulfill all my promises to Him, and by His love, and the power of His resurrection flowing through me, I will follow, and obey Him as long as I live and even unto death. Won't you come and follow Him too, for He is risen. He is risen indeed."

So if grief, doubts, or failures have frustrated and crippled you, come to Him and be made whole again, and go quickly and spread the good news, for He's coming again. Maybe very soon! Your faith, deeply anchored in true facts of real history may well be the means by which many will be persuaded and bravely confess before an unbelieving world, "He is risen, He is risen indeed!"

For Discussion and Reflection

1. Of the three individuals pointed to in this chapter, with which do you most closely identify? Why?

2. Read 1 Corinthians 15. Does this give assurance to any doubt about the truth of the Resurrection that lingers in your soul? Why?

POSTSCRIPT

3. When did the reality of Christ's resurrection first impact you?

4. Considering 1 Corinthians 15:10, who are you by the grace of God? When it comes to your life with God, how do you feel about yourself? How has the grace of God in your regard not been in vain?